THE ART OF RESEARCH

The Art of Research

A GUIDE FOR THE GRADUATE

by

B. E. NOLTINGK, PH. D., F. INST. P., A.M.I.E.E.

Central Electricity Research Laboratories,
Leatherhead (Great Britain)

ELSEVIER PUBLISHING COMPANY
Amsterdam — London — New York — 1965

ELSEVIER PUBLISHING COMPANY
335 JAN VAN GALENSTRAAT, P.O. BOX 211, AMSTERDAM

AMERICAN ELSEVIER PUBLISHING COMPANY, INC.
52 VANDERBILT AVENUE, NEW YORK, N.Y. 10017

ELSEVIER PUBLISHING COMPANY LIMITED
RIPPLESIDE COMMERCIAL ESTATE, BARKING, ESSEX

Preface

The study of *Homo investigans* has a fascination that I find it difficult to escape from. A few years ago I had the temerity to enshrine in writing some thoughts about him and how he should be governed, but I find that there is more to be said. That book was ostensibly addressed to his managers—with the secret hope that some of the managed might also have the curiosity to read it. Now, in the orthodox pyramidal structure, there are far fewer people in the higher echelons than at the bottom, so that a book aimed at the lowlier research worker should have a larger audience —and a wider sales. (I am not sure whether it would depart from truth in the direction of insult or flattery to ascribe this suggestion to my publishers).

My purpose here, then, is to set down some of the considerations which arise when one proposes to undertake research. Some could be called the principles of research; others are too trivial to be dignified with that name, and yet seem worth recording, since this might prevent their having to be learnt by bitter experience. Attention has been paid recently to large questions concerning the organisation of research—whether governmental action should be introduced via this ministry or that—and they are no doubt of great importance. Less consideration is given to questions posed further down the scale, and I have tried to make a contribution in these fields—previously to laboratory organisation and now at the real, working level. I hope that some who are starting a research career will read this book, realising that they know—as I am sure I knew at that stage— more about laws of Nature than about research.

My subject spreads over a wide field. What is written may therefore give the impression of a series of disjointed abstracts. It is in the nature of collected words of advice rather than a tidily developed theme, and for chapter headings I was driven to the *Trusty Serving Men* of Kipling's *Just So Stories*. A good many sections would allow of a great deal of expansion; my survey of the sciences, and, still more, the review of different types of research establishment, are dangerously brief. However, as previously, I would plead that questions are more important than answers, so that if I drive the reader to think out his own answer as a correction and amplification of mine I may even have done better than if I had been right first time myself. Alternatively, I may be accused that many of my remarks are obviosities. My defence to that is that most of the best ideas are obvious once they have been formulated: but many folk have not yet put them into practice.

The book may be thought lighter than the subject warrants, both in Pooh Bear's pounds, shillings and ounces and in the style of writing. Both lightnesses may contribute to easier reading. I, at least, cannot resist the temptation to make my readers wonder sometimes how far my tongue has moved into my cheek. If they enjoy Josie Randall's pictures as much as I did, they will forgive their frivolity.

Some may remark again on the texts appearing above the chapters. I hope this will be recognised, not as irreverent banter, but as an illustration of how the Book, if taken off the shelves and dusted, can be found to contain pithy comments even on week-day matters.

In my last Preface, I disclaimed any indebtedness to other writers. I cannot do this now, since I have been reading as I have written. I have tried to show, in footnotes and Bibliography, the relevant earlier literature that I found of most interest. But I believe that learning research is a sufficient problem to warrant considerable attention, and it is because many points remained unsaid, at least in a concise and readable form, that this book seemed to be justified.

Leatherhead,   B.E.N.
August, 1965

Contents

1. What?

What hath the wise man more than the fool? Eccles. 6:8.

The meaning of 'research'

The word 'research' is currently being used more and more widely. It figures in advertisements for the most ordinary articles; it serves to describe more excitingly the activities of mundane people. To be spoken of as 'research-minded' is almost unqualified praise either for bodies corporate or for the individuals who comprise them. What is this *research* to which we are exhorted and for which the prizes are said to be so great?

In recent usage, there is an implication of a connection with science. Over a couple of centuries, science and her step-brother technology have turned the material world upside down, and it is assumed that the pursuit of research—thought of as the method by which these advances have been made—must bring a share of the dividends for the subject studied. A dictionary definition refers to 'systematic investigation', regardless of whether it is astrophysics, metaphysics, Tutankhamen or tiddlywinks that is being investigated. We are, however, in the good company of Humpty Dumpty if we use words to mean whatever we want, and, for the purpose of this book, we shall loosely and empirically define research as whatever is done in a research department—excluding, of course, traditional occupations such as the manufacture of cigarette lighters and other incidentals. Our deliberations are then unified by their common relevance to the great and growing research industry of the world and to the people who work in it. This industry certainly springs from the wider

1

understanding of the world around us that has been gained in recent years and the general success that has been shown to attend the application of this understanding to our own human purposes.

Two ranges of research

In fact, we can, in principle, identify a piece of research work by a point in a two-coordinate system (Fig. 1). The X-axis ranges

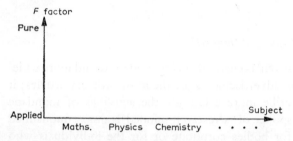

Fig. 1. Two-coordinate description of research.

through the whole list of scientific subjects. The Y-coordinate is a measure of how far the research is pure rather than applied. We may call it the F factor. There are, of course, some forbidden regions: pure aeronautics, for instance, is virtually a contradiction in terms. It is fashionable, and true, to point out the dangers of predicting that there can be no applied science in any particular field. Sir George Thomson* quotes Lord Rutherford as being confident, a mere ten years before Hiroshima, that there would be no Applied Nuclear Physics at high powers. Even Astronomy is beginning to put down leaders from its rarefied atmosphere into the regions of practical application. Perhaps we can be confident that we shall not be troubled by Applied Cosmogony for some years to come.

There is, of course, a great deal of development and application work on behalf of the pure sciences, and the pure scientist may happen to be also a good development engineer. But that is

* G. P. Thomson, Nature of Physics, *Am. J. Phys.*, 28 (1960) 187–192.

2

incidental and we must not confuse subject and object. When people are misguided enough, for instance, to talk about '*Biological Amplifiers*', they do not (for the present) mean that applied biology has reached the stage when amplifiers of desired characteristics can be bred at will and made reproductive, but merely that applied electronics has been used in biology.

The sphere of activity, then, that we call research, stretches on the one hand to the most abstruse attempts to develop comprehensive accounts of Nature, which should unify the description of phenomena in widely separated systems. At the other extreme, it embraces the most mundane production of a gadget to serve a trivial specialised purpose, provided that such a production is approached logically and scientifically.

Each entrant to the research industry has to decide whereabouts in the field he will plough his furrow. Or he fondly thinks he has, though in practice it is likely to be settled for him by his professor or director: his mobility may be limited to edging slightly in one direction or another until he is too old and too senior to do the actual ploughing himself. At least, he has some measure of freedom to select which furrow-planner he will serve under (and complete freedom to select which he will not serve under), so that a brief consideration of the roles of fundamental and applied research may be justified. In practice, of course, this matter is closely related to the type of establishment, as will be considered later.

Fundamental research

The traditional attitude in England has been to maintain the superiority of fundamental research: the purer the higher. Perhaps this can be traced back to the exaggerated Victorian concept that it was unaristocratic to be concerned with improvements in material things. It would be dangerous for the modern researcher to take this superiority for granted; he might find that he was out of step with the newest ideas in the East or the West. Nevertheless, there is a fascination and allurement in fundamental scientific

3

research that can be very compelling. An essential response of the intelligent mind to its surroundings is the attempt to analyse and understand them and to express the impression they make. Man has done this through his art and his philosophy over many centuries. But recently—almost overnight, on the scale of the history of the race—he has found this new method, *Science*, and the exciting novelty about it is that it is cumulative: he can build on what his forbears and his colleagues have already done.

The exhilaration, then, that can be engendered by a successfully accomplished piece of research, is akin to that of the artist or composer. The poet wrestles with his words until at last they are obedient to him and he knows that something of his vision is enshrined in them. He has achieved. The scientist, no less, by his patience and ingenuity in marshalling the factors so that simple conclusions can be drawn from complex data, has achieved— either on paper or at the experimental bench—a specific aim. He, moreover, has a more precise yardstick by which to assess what he has done: he appeals not only to subjective aesthetic judgment, but to the rigid criteria of self-consistency and of value to the march of scientific discovery.

It is not, therefore, surprising that pure science has always its devotees. Those who are gripped by the wonder of the universe around them, possessed of a restless curiosity and a bent to analyse, keen to pit the strength of their minds in siege against the mysteries that have held out longest, confident that new vantage points will lead to conquest, they will find the pursuit of pure science a compelling and inspiring exercise. Perhaps they will need to be longer winded than their colleagues following applied science and technology, for the prizes of pure science, if richer, come in general at longer intervals. The fundamental scientist's work may be applicable to no thing, but it is applicable to everybody; he will be able to publish his discoveries to all the world. He will be untroubled, and unenthused, by prospects of commercial exploitations. His calling is for those with leanings to the cloister rather than the mart.

At those highest ordinates of Fig. 1, the criterion of value, by

4

which a field of research is assessed, is an aesthetic one. The great discoveries are those which widen our knowledge in the most far-reaching manner. As we sink to lower ordinates, another criterion plays an increasing part, namely the likelihood of the results of the research leading to a material advantage. The change is a smooth and continuous one. It is very possible to study some phenomena because they form an interesting facet of Nature, while having the secret hope that in the long run great technological advantages may accrue. It is also perfectly possible to set out with the aim of producing an improved process or device, and, on the way, to establish a basic law.

In fact, *Usefulness* and *Scientific Value* are not necessarily opposed. Fig. 1 ought, therefore, to be replaced by a three-dimensional representation in which these quantities are plotted orthogonally. We can then appreciate the happy state of the scientist working in a field that combines high marks on both counts: he will have honours heaped on him by learned societies and money heaped on him by industry—perhaps!

Applied research

But it will in practice generally be necessary for a man to make a broad choice between scientific interest and material usefulness, between pure and applied. Obviously, the latter emphasis is better suited for folk with the more sharply developed human interest, with a keener enjoyment at seeing their ideas blossom into tangible sequels. It is probably true as a generalisation—but with a number of notable exceptions—to say that the applied scientist must be more of an experimentalist. His academic brother tends to deal with abstract simplified states, whose very simplification makes it possible for his calculations to range further ahead of his experiments; he can choose his own experimental set-up so as to make his mathematics valid. The applied scientist commonly has so many contributory factors entering the practical set-up he is confronted with that only approximate calculations are justified.

5

At the extreme end—of the lowest Fig. 1 ordinates—comes the man who devises new industrial processes or constructs new apparatus. In the limit, he is a pure engineer, exploiting existing knowledge rather than throwing up fresh knowledge. He, of course, must find his satisfaction in the application and embodiment of principles rather than the principles themselves. We shall have more to say later about that elusive but important quality, creativity, but it is fair to suggest that while the brilliant engineer needs some creative streak, his more average colleague will do plenty of sound and useful work without it.

The tendency towards 'application'

With considerations such as these in mind, the research worker has to plan his career. It is worth remembering that for each individual there is almost invariably a tendency to move in the direction from fundamental towards applied work. Several factors combine to bring this about. As a man's career progresses, he gains in practical working experience; but more often than not, he is actually losing familiarity—except in one or two narrow fields—with the broad basis of facts and theories that he amassed at college. Such an exchange of knowledge fits him better for applied than for basic work, especially if a change of subject—a shift along the abscissae of Fig. 1—is involved. The concentrated absorption of basic information during college days is very difficult to parallel later in life and in a rapidly developing field may give an irretrievable advantage to the recent graduate compared with a competitor who has been moved along from research in another topic. Perhaps the development of much more extensive postgraduate courses in a re-organised educational system will change the situation. Again, there appears to be a trough in university recruitment practice, at least in England. Precise figures are not available, but a general impression is that if we plot P_i, defined as the probability that a new appointee has come from an extra-university position, against the level he goes to in a university science department, we shall find a curve as in Fig. 2.

6

This could be combined with P_0, the probability that the job university personnel move to from that grade is non-academic to

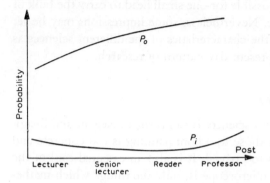

Fig. 2. Probabilities of university staff moving to and from non-academic posts.

show that there is a net exodus from academic life. Since higher F factors (Fig. 1) are found inside than outside universities the broad result is a negative slope dF/dt. In case the thesis needs further labouring, consider the situation of a research administrator allotting tasks to his staff. He could well say: "Dr. Deep's understanding of basic phenomena will fit him to elucidate what is happening in this bit of troublesome technology", but he could scarcely argue that Mr. Broad's familiarity with the details of certain machines would given him much of a start in unravelling the obscure principles which must contribute to their functioning. The practical conclusion from our arguments is that the far-sighted career-planner will set his personal course a little to fundamental of where he really wishes to be, remembering this inevitable tendency to drift down-wind application-wards.

Scientific disciplines

A thorough survey of the content of the various subjects we have spread out along the abscissae of Fig. 1 would be somewhat

7

beyond the scope of this book—it would form a good working alternative to the Encyclopedia Brittanica. It would also be far beyond the compass of one author's learning: the days are long past when it was possible for one small head to carry the bulk of human knowledge. Nevertheless, some impressions may be set down of some of the characteristics of the different sciences as they fall into the present-day pattern of research.

Mathematics

Mathematics is not a science. It can form an elegant and imaginative exercise for those to whom painting is too concrete and crossword puzzles too trivial. It is also an essential tool of the scientist, just as a microscope is, only the things which mathematics allows to be measured, and the details which it brings to light are abstract rather than material ones. Our empirical definition of research (p. 1) however, would easily include the work of the mathematician within its orbit, for he is one of the oldest inhabitants of laboratories.

Sometimes there is the impression that he can be kept as a priest of the oracle, to make an infallible pronouncement on the infrequent occasions when he is consulted, but normally to be ignored while the scientist gets on with the real work. This approach seldom seems to work in practice, since it is found that, apart from the simplest cases, the mathematics cannot be considered in isolation. A rigorous formulation and evaluation of a real problem is practically never possible and the decision over what approximations are profitable and permissible requiries such a full understanding of the problem that before he takes it the mathematician must be or become a scientist himself.

The practical corollary is that most disciples of mathematics are ill-advised if they interpret their discipline too narrowly. They should expect—uncobblerlike—to desert their lasts, so th they can play a more central part in some work of their laborato even though their services as masseurs also remain genera available for figure manipulation.

8

One practical advantage that the mathematician possesses is his independence of apparatus—though this is becoming undermined by growing reliance on calculators or computers. It follows that his activities cannot be curbed by restrictions on capital expenditure, a form of control that often proves most exasperating to experimentalists. It also gives him increased scope for exercising an interest in his colleagues' fields; so often, the flash of what might be a clever idea is not followed up, just because the only individual who could easily mount the necessary experiment is preoccupied with other matters and it would seem an excessive intrusion for the originator of the idea to insist on assembling the necessary equipment himself. But if the experiment consists of a couple of hours spent checking various re-arrangements of assorted equations, no-one will know unless it proves successful, and then it cannot be argued against. Such an approach is especially useful for a senior man, whose juniors will often welcome his examining theoretical issues where they would resent any detailed interference at a practical level.

Engineering

Engineering, strictly speaking, is no more a science than mathematics is. Its prime function is to utilise in a systematic manner the discoveries that have been made by science. Engineering, however, impinges on research laboratories in two ways. Firstly, much of the apparatus of the modern scientist is so complex, while so much of his success depends on extracting the utmost information from it, that the apparatus needs to be professionally designed and even professionally modified and nurtured. The scientist must often, therefore, have an engineer playing an honourable but secondary role to him.

Secondly, in the lower values of the F factor to which we keep referring, we find a large body of what may be termed *Engineering research*. Broadly speaking, this means investigations into obscure conditions that are found in engineering systems; it may quite correctly be called applied research. Now it can be argued that an engineering training does not equip a man for research; it is designed to engender in him a respect for the formulae of the past and a healthy conservatism based on a realisation of his responsibilities. This is not readily compatible with the precocious questioning of fundamentals and the passion to uncover something new that form the life blood of research. Indeed, it might be mischievously suggested that pre-occupation with research is evidence of unbalance in engineering education. A surprising amount of the research done in University Engineering Departments could equally appropriately be done in Physics Departments. But it would be going too far to insist that all the engineers' research should be done for them by physicists and chemists. In some projects, the technological background carries such weight that an investigator with a thorough knowledge of it may acquit himself better than one who has concentrated only on fundamentals. And of course there are many who would call themselves engineers who have combined with their profession much of the training and most of the outlook of the purer scientist.

Those who are debating as to what field they shall do their research in (though, unfortunately, the die is often cast too early in their careers, certainly before their education is completed by reading this book!) will note that engineering research is necessarily less fundamental. An engineering qualification, however, leaves a particularly wide variety of occupations open to those possessing it, from severely practical short-term activities guiding day-to-day projects, through assorted administrative responsibilities, to long-term wide ranging research. Perhaps it is fair to suggest that in an ideal world engineers would concentrate more in the direction of the first two activities, leaving research as such increasingly to the basic scientists.

Physics

Physics has cleverly manoeuvred itself into a monopoly position where practically the whole of science is counted as physics, with the exception of those fields that have been parcelled out to other disciplines. Thus, while chemistry used to reckon that it embraced things that happened on the smallest known material scale, molecular and inter-atomic, confining physics to the more macroscopic, Rutherford and his colleagues neatly leap-frogged chemistry and planted the flag of physics in the smallest world of all, that of nucleons and electrons. There is an obverse to the story of omnivorous physics. As the ramifications of applied physics have spread wider and wider, it has cast off new branches of engineering to specialise in fuller detail in the new applications that have become possible. Radio engineering, electronic engineering, nuclear engineering and control engineering all deal with matters that started, fairly recently, as physics. The light touch of physics disinclines it to linger when repeated practical applications are demanding the accumulation of elaborate information that would be uninteresting if it were not useful.

The rate at which new branches of applied physics are being started is increasing. This suggests that many folk now receiving their formal training will apply their knowledge, later in their careers, to techniques that are not at present dreamed about. For such novelties, physics, claiming to be the most fundamental science, is an obviously sound preparation.

An unfortunate trend over the years has been towards a sharp division between *theoretical* and *experimental* physics. Presumably the vast extent of the experimental facts that must be absorbed, and the complexity of the mathematical techniques in which a theoretician must be competent, prevent them both being learnt at once. The human inclination to do those things which can be done well and omit the operations that are less skillfully performed has tended to concentrate scientists into two streams. The one group can handle data but is ill at ease when confronted with the actual hardware for conducting experiments; the others realise the idiosyncrasies of their apparatus and can coax it into performing consistently, but find difficulty in drawing the more obscure conclusions from the results and sometimes in designing the most profitable experiments. All scientists are exposed to this danger—

we have emphasised the parallel situation for the mathematician —but it is perhaps most severe for the physicist. Let him guard against it as he can by broadening the basis of his training; then he will remain in the true stream of scientific tradition, based on the interplay of experiment and theory.

Chemistry

Despite the sharp practice that we have remarked on in defining the frontier between physics and chemistry, the latter is still an enormous subject. There are, in fact, considerably more practising chemists than physicists in the world. This is because the scientific development of industry has reached the rather easier stage at which chemistry can be applied almost universally to its materials, while the more fundamental and more diverse applications of physics are only beginning. We may expect that the numerical preponderance will be reversed, as is presaged by statistics from the schools: perhaps we can confirm the prediction from the saying that World War I was a war of the chemists, World War II of the physicists; for martial industry is commonly a stage ahead of civil.

Continuing to compare chemistry with physics—since they are sufficiently alike in many features to compete for the allegiance of many embryonic scientists—it would appear at the lower levels that chemistry consists much more of arbitrary facts that must be learned by rote because they are not susceptible to being reasoned out. This may be a reflection on our syllabuses and our teaching techniques. In any case it disappears with deeper understanding of the subject.

Perhaps it is fair to say that chemistry is the field for the man who likes to have his terms of reference well defined. His instructions are: "Synthesise this" or "Analyse that" rather than: "Look into this phenomenon to see if you can make sense of it or exploit it".

The relations between chemists and other sciences are not symmetrical. While many of those trained in other disciplines would almost pride themselves on their chemical ignorance, the chemist himself must have a fair knowledge of physics to understand his own subject, and at least a smattering of electronics in order rightly to believe or disbelieve many of his own instruments. He should beware of deceiving himself into thinking that he knows all about either.

Biology

Perhaps to the biologist, biology is a word that has much too wide a coverage to be used for a single science. Certainly to the outsider it appears to cleave sharply into two halves that are the prerogatives of the laboratory men and the naturalists respectively. Considering the qualities of temperament required in the scientists, this is surely a sharper division than the mere separation into two kingdoms having botanists and zoologists as their subjects. Yet engineers and applied physicists have also their field work, and for many experimenters the alternation between home laboratory and external site is a strong attraction of the work. Not only does it relieve the monotony of the laboratory (and complementarily alleviate the discomfort of the field) but it serves as an acted reminder that the findings of abstract science are really being applied to the real world.

Biology has been traditionally described as a descriptive science. Its proportionately larger number of feminine protagonists was said to accord with their greater imaginative powers and lesser facility in quantitative work. Currently, however, biology's inexactness as a science is being matched by growing development of an inexact mathematics; much recent growth in statistics can be traced back to the needs—often self-met—of the biologists. Simultaneously, in biophysics and biochemistry, newer offspring have been growing, that inherit some of the precision of their other parents.

13

"The output from our teaching hospitals is spread from offices, through the army, into research laboratories; they are G.P.s, dons, coroners and missionaries"

Medicine

Medicine, no doubt, might be considered a subject on its own. The great majority of its practitioners, however, would regard themselves not as scientists but artists, not experimenting but applying, and with a large leavening of the humanities in their training and their working. It may be noted, incidentally, that a medical qualification provides the entry to an even wider diversity of openings than does engineering. The output from our teaching hospitals is spread from offices, through the army, into research laboratories; they are G.P.'s, dons, coroners and missionaries. Moreover, a powerful trade union has done much to ensure an ample remuneration—apart from the anomalous initiation period. Another almost unique feature of the profession is that, at least in surgery, a man can climb to the very peak of eminence without having to forsake the exercising of his personal manual dexterity; those saddened at abandoning, during working hours, every tool except the pen and the dictaphone may well counsel dexterous youth to pay heed to this.

But once the medico has entered, and been absorbed by, the research laboratory, his life is little different from that of any other inmate.

Sociology

From biology and medicine, studying Man as an organism, we may turn to the social sciences studying him as a gregarious animal —to the naturalists observing Nature in her most extravagant outreach. All new sciences are viewed askance by those of the established orders, and this has been repeated for sociology. Perhaps it is the absence of a large body of established facts, whose memorising forms much of the discipline of scientific apprenticeship, that basically distinguishes a new science. It means that there is less to hold up the progress of an imaginative campaigner; it also means that it is more difficult to detect the charlatan.

There is a subconscious tendency to make the social sciences an ideological battlefield. On the one hand are those who believe

"The naturalists observing Nature in her most extravagant outreach"

in the onward march of a Science whose application to the whole gamut of human activities offers the one hope of salvation for mankind. They will rejoice in this invasion by scientists of territory formerly occupied only by humanities-trained administrators. They will anticipate that scientific diagnosis and prescription will give the solution to all social evils: to know all is not merely to forgive all, but to cure all. Opposing them will be the believers—perhaps in a barely formulated creed—that man is not in his totality amenable to scientific analysis. Whether the belief stems from a sense of the logically unsatisfactory concept of a self-analysable machine, or whether it is based on a blunt conviction that science is not omnipotent, it suggests limits to what can be achieved by the social sciences—or by psychology; but few would maintain that those limits were yet being approached. There is still scope for much exploration, with hopes of quick returns in human betterment—and risks of laboriously established obviosities.

Planned specialisation

Having flitted along the abscissae of Fig. 1 using a very small scale map, we may change to a larger scale and pay some attention to the question of sub-divisions within a subject.

For the great majority of scientists, the broad bounds of their specialisation are settled with, or even before graduation. Within those bounds, there is more opportunity for selecting a field. Or is there? For while most recruiting boards profess to favour a candidate with clear ideas as to his aims, in practice, everywhere but in the academic world, the junior will have his research topic appointed by a more experienced senior. There are, however, two ways in which the rigour of this situation is softened.

Firstly, within his terms of reference, there will almost certainly be manoeuvring room to allow the exercise of considerable choice. It is right for a scientist to pay some (though not exclusive) attention to which approach will suit his temperament better, because he has an increased chance of success along that line. If ordered, for instance, to study the effects of lightning flashes on *Drosophila*, our budding bio-physicist could be a naturalist, an empiricist, an electro-technologist or many other things. He can work strictly within his terms of reference, and still, with luck, indulge his own fancy. Secondly, the junior would be working for a poor boss if the latter paid no attention to the expressed wishes of his scientist; rather should a large contributory factor in his shaping of programmes be the utilisation of the skills and preferences of his team. Therefore, it behoves all embarking on research to consider carefully the details of subject that they will seek to pursue. University staff may steer directly for it; workers elsewhere may find the need for long tacks.

A few research workers may have been born, or at least reared with a burning sense of vocation for one narrow field. They are the exceptions: most preferences arise quite casually from chance encounters. Most youngsters interviewed will be found to vote that the one topic which they have in any way met previously is the most worth-while subject to pursue. Another often repeated experience is that a subject, which had appeared dull and forbidding when viewed from afar, proves to have a wealth of interest in it once the motivation for studying it has arisen because a widening orbit has given that subject a personal relevance and application.

From all this, it may be concluded that it is, in fact, up to a scientist to select deliberately and rationally what his target speciality shall be. He should be aided and abetted in this by his immediate senior. The target may, of course, be a moving one. Our plea is simply that thought should be given to it—though not so much as to detract from concentration on the current technical task.

At any one period, certain scientific fields attract much more attention than others, partly, no doubt, because the time is ripe for advances to be made there, but also partly just because they are fashionable. Two opposite reactions to this are possible. A man may say that he wants to be in the main stream of development, so as to be a fellow-specialist with the mighty; he will despise all side-alleys and backwaters. Alternatively, he may reflect that that part of the scientific frontier is well manned, not to say congested, so that only the very brilliant will be able to achieve eminence there; accordingly he will elect to study a more neglected field, with a larger chance of becoming a world authority in a smaller way. Wark* recommends fashionable fields for the 'near first-class', others for the first-class, but it may be dangerous to be dogmatic: probably each should make his choice according to his temperament. The happiest person, of course, is the one who selected today's fashion to specialise in yesterday.

Curves of knowledge

To develop this theme, it is helpful to use the concept of curves of knowledge, which we introduced in a previous publication. Referring to Fig. 3a, we find a graph, on which, in principle, the level of anyone's knowledge can be depicted. As in Fig. 1, the abscissae represent subjects, for instance Maths., Physics, Chemistry...; the ordinates correspond to degree of knowledge in the appropriate subject. We could mark in G.C.E. "O" Level and "A" Level, and we might distinguish the curves corresponding to graduation from different universities. However, it is more precise to recognise that the curve is really a histogram with essentially discrete steps in the X-direction; we can then (very much in principle!) define the Y-co-ordinate as the number of words (unpadded) that can be written on the subject given as the X-co-ordinate. This allows the demonstration of the deficiencies that are all too familiar in real-life— a curve that appears full and well-rounded on a small scale, but which shows ominous cracks and omissions when plotted to a large scale.

Our scientist, then, will leave college with a relatively broad curve, say G; he will, if the educational reformers are successful, have left school with an even broader curve, S. Omnivorous student days may have equipped him with isolated peaks of

* I. W. WARK, Scientific Research as a Career, *Nature*, 197 (1963) 737–740.

knowledge far away from science—in saxophony or philately or theology. Once, however, he embarks on a research career, he will tend to throw up a spike of knowledge on a very narrow front. The vital question he must face is whether or not he will accept the confinement of his activities within this spike.

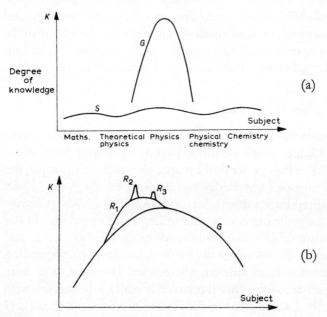

Fig. 3. Curves of knowledge.

It should be noted that there is a natural tendency for the spike to become spikier as time goes on. For one thing, the scientist's general background will dwindle as memories of past learning fade. At the same time, as fresh facets of the new subject are revealed, one narrow aspect is likely to be pursued primarily, and the limit of his learning here driven further and further out. This is on the assumption that the X-scale has remained constant while the research has continued; the real triumph is when the scale has to be expanded to cope with the discoveries the scientist has made. Thus, under the subject of 'Bats', there would, until

20

a few years ago, have been only a brief sub-title 'Blind Guidance'. Subsequently, Griffin has added 'Ultrasonic Echo-location' to be sub-divided into such sections as 'Carrier Frequency', 'Pulse Repetition Frequency', 'Intensity'. More recently still, the further divisions of 'Receiver Signal' and 'Extraction of Information' have to be included. Freud might have claimed the distinction of adding the whole subject of Therapeutic Psycho-analysis to the abscissae; some might suggest that Eysenck had the greater distinction of deleting it again.

Changing specialisation

Thus most research workers will tend, if undisturbed, to specialise, to keep in one subject, sometimes returning to redeem their (and the world's) ignorance in a closely neighbouring subject, but never departing far from their original theme. As depicted in Fig. 3b, (which can be seen to have an expanded scale compared with 3a), they will extend their graduate's curve of knowledge G, first to R_1, then to R_2, and then, perhaps, to R_3.

We can identify an individual's speciality as that subject which has, for him, the maximum value of dK/dt. We can assume that there will be only one maximum. In some cases a scientist might maintain that he was simultaneously interested in several distinct growing points, but it is difficult to believe that he would not need, for all but one of them, juniors who would be the real working scientists at their own subjects: the singleminded attention needed for real progress in research can scarcely be devoted to two different subjects at once.

It is interesting to consider how these growing-points—the subjects corresponding to $(dK/dt)_{max}$—may vary with time. The history of the more usual case we have described in Fig. 3b is depicted in Fig. 4a, where we have rotated the abscissae of Fig. 3 to become the ordinates, in order to give time its conventional place along the X-axis. Two broad alternatives to this type of behaviour can be distinguished, shown in Figs. 4b and 4c. In the former, the research worker is uprooted boldly on one or more occasions and transplanted to another field. In Fig. 4c, a more gradual process is shown, whereby his main interest is shifted steadily in a certain direction, so that he finds after a few years he has a different primary concern although no abrupt transitions have taken place. It cannot be said that any one of the three approaches is a unique best. To a first approximation, the purer

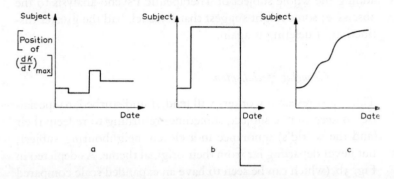

Fig. 4. Changes of speciality with time.

scientist will be type (a), but by 'pure scientist' we do not mean a worker in pure science so much as a man whose love of any science is untainted by a love of administration. Type (c), and perhaps still more (b) might be expected to fit a man better for pinnacles of responsibility, where he will supervise the work of others working in fields a little remote from his own current themes and where a wider experience would provide a better background for judgments. The high road to responsibility, however, does not run so simply and logically from a departure point of generalisation. For the man who has moved from one subject to another too quickly will never have reached the public eye—or even the eyes of those mighty in science—as a knowledge-able worker at one topic before he has jumped to the next. So the ambitious climber is well-advised to persist for several years as an expert along one line: if he has been successful here, this will give him an introduction to high places, and he will often find that those he meets there will assume, perhaps rashly, that his expertise in one field will qualify him for leadership in another. He should, therefore, also keep himself generally educated on a broad front in preparation for what the future may bring forth.

That the need for a wide-reaching liaison is no new phenomenon is brought out in a quotation recently made by S. A. Bergen*: "Most of the work still to be done in science and the useful arts is precisely that which needs the knowledge and co-operation of many scientists—that is why it is necessary for scientists and technologists to meet—even in those branches of knowledge which seem to have least relation and connection with one another". The quotation is from Antoine Lavoisier in 1793.

In summary, let research workers keep wide interests as much as they can. This will sometimes be by being concerned successively with very different problems, but even when they persist in one direction for long periods, they must not close their minds to the rest of the world. The all-too-prevalent attitude: "This is not relevant to my current work; I cannot afford to take notice of it" is a vicious one.

Other interests

Akin to this issue of how narrowly specialist a research worker should be is the question of what proportion of his time should be devoted to research. Certainly we believe that a scientist—as anyone else—should normally have a full life, with many interests outside his laboratory, although in the short view this may impede his progress compared with those restricted to closer horizons. But even within his laboratory there is scope for considerable diversification. The association of teaching and research at a university is commonly justified by explaining that the teaching will lose much of its freshness and enthusiasm if it is separated from the source of new knowledge, but in fact teaching can confer reciprocal benefits on research. This is partly because the discipline of explaining ideas to others demands a clarity in the

---

* S. A. BERGEN, *J. Inst. Elec. Engrs. (London)*, 9 (1963) 470.

mind of the formulator that can scarcely be achieved otherwise. It is also—and this is the point we would stress—because of the need most people have for an alternation of activity. Research work more than most involves long sterile periods when little inspiration is to be gained from the results that are not successfully accruing. Most research workers would be well advised to cultivate deliberately some occupation that will help to carry them through these periods. As a man grows in responsibility, of course, he often finds that he has an interest in other projects beyond his own first love, and this can soften the intensity of depressions. Again, if he is at all minded that way, he should welcome the occasional administrative chore, be it advice to a training panel or service on a canteen committee: those who impose these chores may note that their value, in this connection, is greater if the work they involve is not tied to too rigid a timetable. For many, however, this line of defence against frustration will come in the broad field of education. Sometimes, in the simple teaching of those on lower rungs of the ladder; by corollary, this is an argument in favour of having some instructional courses on laboratory premises. Sometimes, in a commercial organisation, by answering relatively mundane enquiries: we are suggesting that the information service should not be entirely separated from the research laboratory. Sometimes as the preparation of a survey paper covering his own and neighbouring subjects. This last, we would maintain, should always be at least in the background thinking of researchers; it will encourage them to be specialists, making themselves world experts qualified to write authoritatively on at least one topic; it will make them generalists in that they will come to see the context in which their own work is set. By means such as these, a small proportion of a scientist's time—perhaps 10%—can usefully be employed away from the main stream of his work, affording a guard against frustration by allowing some sense of achievement even when there has been no positive output from his own research.

Unlearnt skills

We may conclude this chapter of *What?* with a brief section on *What Not?* Here we will list, not a series of warnings about those actions most fraught with danger in the scientific world, but some of the mental equipment which is likely not to have been provided during his formal training and whose absence the new research worker may well regret. Thus forewarned, he can aim, as opportunity presents, at mental forearmament.

Workshop practice

Scientific training is beginning to embrace a larger component of elementary practical skills but it still has a long way to go to the optimum. Most scientists would find it a great asset to be possessed of a much greater familiarity with workshop practice than they have gained in their passage along the conveyor belt of the *Equal Opportunities Educational System*. Unless they have prejudiced their university entrance prospects by lingering over-long in the garage or beside the model aeroplane, their acquaintance with machines and machining will have the superficiality associated with an unexamined subject. This will handicap them later on, partly because they will want to do some workmanlike constructional operations themselves, partly because it will make it more difficult to gain a feeling for the simple mechanical design that enters into a majority of experiments, and perhaps most because an unnecessary barrier has arisen thereby between the scientist and the technician.

Materials

Closely parallel to ignorance over fabrication techniques is an ignorance about the materials to be fabricated. There is a risk that the research worker will think that fatigue has much more to do with dislocations than with his choice of an alloy for an important structural member. I can recall that, as a student, I only learned one of the properties of cast iron just after I had thrown a casting

25

"Perhaps the budding scientist can set himself idle but imaginative sums in his bath"

across the room; I suppose I had drawn conclusions from the assumption that a cast iron case was one that would not fall apart if suddenly put to the test. Neither ignorance over fabrication nor ignorance over materials are easily remedied, for both are practical matters requiring extended practical experience; but the newly fledged scientist can at least be alert to accept any opportunities that may present themselves for filling such gaps in his knowledge.

Orders of magnitude

Another, rather different subject at which the recruit will find himself very short of practice may be termed *Order-of-Magnitude Arithmetic*. Most of the calculations he has done in his younger days will have produced answers with at least three significant figures; these answers would have been called faulty if the last figures were wrong just as much as if the accompanying power of ten were several units in error. Real life in a laboratory is often different. On many occasions there, schemes will present themselves for assessment whose feasibility does not turn on accuracies of a few per cent but on accuracies of a few orders of magnitude. Indeed, the data on which the schemes are based are probably only crude approximations. What is required of the calculator is complete reliability that gross errors have been eliminated, an awareness of what is questionable within the broad limits of accuracy assigned, the ability to produce from memory or from the handbook the necessary constants, and, if possible, an action rapid enough to prevent much time being wasted in chasing fruitless dreams. These are rare facilities to possess. Perhaps examiners could seek to inculcate them by framing novel questions to be answered in a time that is too short for thoroughness. Perhaps the budding scientist can set himself idle but imaginative sums in his bath.

Librarianship

In schooldays, a pupil is encouraged to think it almost useless to know where to look up a forgotten fact: for examination purposes, he either has the fact in his memory or it is useless. In college, there is some improvement on this, but when earning his living by his science, the ex-pupil will find that almost the exact opposite is true. It is no use remembering a fact unless he can also remember where he learnt it. For he will never trust his memory with sufficient certainty—or if he does, other people will not. It is therefore essential to develop a considerable proficiency at librarianship—more, unless he is very lucky, than his official tutors will have taught. Familiarity with published material should range over books on fringe subjects, gaining an idea how to skim through them to extract the essential information, whether it is so elementary that he does not want to admit his ignorance or whether it is so recent that its combination with an idea in another field would be revolutionary. Familiarity should include a knowledge of which journals bear on the speciality taken up and how to use abstracting services. Familiarity should even have bred an element of contempt! since an instinctive respect for the printed word makes it difficult for most people to appreciate that it is occasionally completely false. Such wisdom is not difficult to come by, provided a consious effort is made to cultivate it.

English

A plea which is often uttered is that the scientist should pay more attention to studying one subject already supposed to feature on his curriculum, namely the writing of English. We are not concerned here to give much instruction in how that should be done—other (mutually contradictory?) pens have taken that up— but with listing the subject as a likely deficiency in a research worker's repertoire. However, it may be worth emphasising a point that has been made elsewhere*. At the stage of starting

---

* M. MILBOURN, The Requirements of Industry for Physicists, *The Institute of Physics Bulletin,* 11 (1960) 331.

research, there is normally a sudden reversal of roles. When a student writes, as part of his training, he writes for those more expert than himself; he is trying to impress them that he also is possessed of quite a large proportion of their superior knowledge. On the other hand, a research worker should himself be at the frontiers of knowledge in his own small field and must therefore be writing for those knowing less than he does. A basically different approach is consequently needed, starting far back at the fundamentals where writer and reader have a common knowledge, and this may come hardly to those who have been diligently schooled to write only for greater experts.

Another protest I would voice at current scientific styles of writing, concerns the growing tendency to use nouns adjectivally. Perhaps because so much reading never gets beyond headlines, a form of writing is adopted in which prepositions are ignored (although we have a rich selection of them in English) and a chain of nouns strung together in an inelegant and often ambiguous manner. I must found a *Society for the Preservation of Prepositions.*

2. Where?

*Where shall wisdom be found? and where
is the place of understanding?*

Job. 28:12.

As well as deciding what shall be the subject of his research, the research worker must decide where to do it. The two questions are, of course, inter-related. Indeed, the chief reason for opting to work at any particular place is the facility it will provide for undertaking certain things in company with certain other people: *What?* and *Who?* may over-ride *Where?* There are, however, some matters which are best raised in considering location.

My grandmother once recounted to me how she had operated the bellows in the family stable, and by most accounts the discoveries which ensued were of a high standard. But that was a long time ago, and my grandfather was above the ordinary run of metallurgists. Very few people today can engage seriously in science without the backing of an establishment large enough to furnish them with (and to furnish!) a laboratory.

As we considered under '*What*' the range of subjects that a research worker might investigate, so we consider under '*Where*' the variety of establishments at which he can work. A similar warning must be uttered that no individual can have had sufficient experience to discuss them thoroughly, yet a sketch of potential assets and potential dangers may at least suggest points to watch out for when selecting one type of laboratory rather than another; admittedly there is a risk that bad sampling will have led to false conclusions. A wide variation always occurs between individual cases, but it does seem possible to pick out certain generic tendencies.

30

To the outsider, a university science departmeut often appears an ideal setting for research work. A large element of freedom may be expected in choosing both the subject to be tackled and the energy to be put into it. It will be easy, indeed unavoidable, to meet the great ones both in one's own field and in the neighbouring disciplines that are sometimes so tantalisingly relevant. There is a sense in which awkward human situations in university laboratories are more readily self-adjusting, since one university resembles another to an extent that facilitates transfer; a junior is reckoned as bringing credit rather than disloyalty if he moves to a more senior post elsewhere.

On the other hand, universities seem chronically impoverished —for revenue if not for large capital items. The time saved on administrative chores, because freedom reduces the need for organisational tidiness, may well, therefore, be lost by lack of labour-saving devices and labour-saving people. It has been queried, too, whether university departments are sometimes unjustifiably professor-dominated: the fact that the formal chain of command is less rigid than in other more highly organised establishments does not always prevent the exercise of considerable power that may be the more tyrannical because it is concealed. Universities often voice complaints that they cannot attract staff of the right calibre, and there may certainly be problems in achieving the rate of expansion envisaged in the Robbins report. But perhaps this is just because of the very high standards called for. There is a general impression abroad in the rest of the research world that universities are good places to move to, which suggests that they must offer an attractive career.

Colleges of Advanced Technology are at present still very much feeling their way. They must present some opportunities for launching adventurous new projects, but the general impression conveyed is of an initial (no doubt correct) preoccupation with teaching, that serves to emphasise the difficulty of research work flourishing without a certain atmosphere of tradition.

31

Civil service

Employment in a branch of the Scientific Civil Service offers great security and a very sound career. The distinctive features of work there arise mainly because a passion for uniformity and precision—said to be necessitated by public accountability—has brought into existence an effective, but vast administrative machine. The machine does not occasion much inconvenience, because the Service has been in existence a long time, changing comparatively slowly; this has allowed a running-in period, during which those asperities that occasioned the most severe friction have been eliminated, or means found for circumventing them.

In some parts of the Civil Service, fundamental research is prosecuted. The impression may be given by some of these that the pace of working is much more leisurely than outside—not necessarily wrongly, because there are some things that must be done slowly and thoroughly. A larger proportion of Civil Service effort is geared to specific technological objectives, which bring their own incentive to urgency. Rule by committee is in danger of becoming excessive. That may not be inherent in the system, rather is it the result of much of the work being on large projects: the economical co-ordination of any project that is too big for one man to assimilate all its details, and at the same time so advanced as to depend critically on those details, is still largely an unsolved problem.

Research associations

Over-ruling by committees is a greater danger in research associations. It is an obviously attractive idea to set up a body to undertake research for a whole industry: overlapping is avoided, and those firms that are too small to afford the minimum outlay for a worthwhile group of scientists can pool their resources. Some of the dangers that must be avoided by research associations are less publicised. There will be a tendency, for instance, for individual firms to try to retain for themselves the projects that they regard as really worthwhile. At the same time, they will protest if the association undertakes too much that could be regarded as idly academic. Only a narrow space is left between, therefore, in which to look for good research subjects. Moreover, impartiality must be preserved between the interests of the numerous sponsoring firms, and it may have been ruled that this must be safeguarded through the oversight of multi-membered committees. This is the great danger in the life of a research association: that its affairs should be controlled in much too great detail by a gathering where 'political' interests jostle technical ones, and some, at least, are attending because there is not much demand for their time and services within their own organisation.

Another danger is that of pay scales not keeping pace with inflation; the staff are too few to be organised effectively, and there is no large employer to judge directly the profitability of his scientists. The general opinion is held that work should not be restricted, and so the outlay goes, probably unrealised, on more, but cheaper men.

But with all these dangers, there is an opportunity to make a considerable impact on the industry served. Many who have chafed at being chivvied from one short term project to another by their employer have longed for just this sort of chance to step back and examine things more thoroughly. Probably in a research association the director is even more important than in other laboratories; since the association has been carved out of nothing, its staff will tend to have less motivating loyalties and will depend on their director for coherence as well as for protection against other would-be shapers of their programmes.

Private industry

For people employed by a single, private firm, committees are not much menace. Another attraction of this section of industry is the prospect of the possibility—if a faint one—of influencing large issues: purse strings are controlled by individuals, who may be accessible, instead of by Acts of Parliament, which certainly are not. However, in industry, there is also an increased risk—larger than is often admitted—of insecurity. Observers' memories are shorter than the disruption caused to victims, but outright redundancies are not unknown. Confrontation with removal to distant parts or with work at uncongenial tasks as the only alternatives to redundancy are more common. Admittedly, the highest salaries, paid to the highest scientists in industry are very high, but to offset this, there are many that are far from generous.

In general, industrial work tends to be much more applied. A correlation will be found between the size of the firm and its ability to sponsor fundamental work. It might be suggested that industrial concerns with annual turnovers less than some £ 100 million are unlikely, in the present climate of commercial thought, to maintain genuine fundamental research laboratories. Hard-headed businessmen will regard such laboratories as luxuries and be unwilling to vote them more than a negligible sum of money. Equating the maximum negligible quantity (say 0.1% of turnover) with the minimum viable size of an independent laboratory (order of 50 people at overall cost of £ 2,000 p.a. per head) gives us this figure. Again, the stability and continuity essential to long-term research work are dependent on a financial inertia that comes only with a large concern—and all too rarely, even then. Yet another argument is that only in the industrial juggernauts will the management be thinking far enough ahead for basic research to have any relevance to their planning. Therefore, the innocent recruit should beware; if he is offered employment on fundamental research by too small a concern, the situation is liable to be unstable and short-lived. Moreover, similar reasoning applies all the way down the size range: the smaller the employer, the smaller is likely to be the F factor (in our Fig. 1) of the research work he will ask for. This is not to denigrate such work; there are many exciting compensations of short-term development activities. We merely state that the would-be pure researcher should seek work, if not from government or academic circles, only from very large firms.

If we are trying to answer the literal question *Where?*—and decide on the optimum location of the laboratory where a scientist should seek to work, there are, of course, a multiplicity of personal issues to be settled. Here, we would content ourselves with emphasising the advantage of having the geographical specification of the work-place match that of the home and leisure-time pursuits so as to avoid the need for excessive travelling. It is strange how resigned men can get to sacrificing an appalling proportion of their lives to mere locomotion from one point to another; I even recall one man who seemed proud of travelling right across London to work and was quite scornful of his colleagues who journeyed a trivial five or ten miles. But most scientists—if not people with less creative tasks—will find their days and their tempers both distressingly short: the simple expedient of mini-mising travel helps to lengthen both.

The matter is the more important because of the difficulty of effecting a change. The Americans appear to find it a much lighter matter to uproot themselves and resettle a thousand miles away (of course they have undergone natural selection for this very characteristic). East of the Atlantic, removal is still upheaval. Within the seven ages of man, an individual is likely to find suc-cessively that courtship, house purchase, continuity of schooling and senile conservatism will preclude his moving home. So he must seize promptly on opportunities which arise in the brief intervals between these states. At the same time, he should score heavily in favour of a location for a home, and therefore for a laboratory, which will be accessible to a number of other es-tablishments in case he should later wish to sample their delights. This normally reduces the otherwise considerable attractions of a remotely situated workplace. Similar questions, of course, arise for many professional men. The situation is, perhaps, rather more acute for a scientist, since in most cases he will wish to widen his experience by working at more than one place, while research establishments are sufficiently few and far between that he cannot expect to find one in convenient reach of any arbitrarily chosen home.

Importance of neighbours

So much for the external *Where?* The internal *Where?* ranges over many features of laboratory planning. There are straight-forward physical aspects, exemplified in the college where the high-resolution spectroscope only gave of its best when it was no longer next-door neighbour to the women's common room. Such matters might seem obvious, but it is surprising how few people seem to realise, for instance, the propensity of research chemists for leaving taps running. (I speak with feeling from the memory of a basement room in which the resultant series of floods were only eased by a merciful canalisation above the ceiling, giving, while the bowl-shaped light shade was being filled, a period of grace in which to mount the stairs and chide the tenants above). Perhaps all laboratory architects should do vacation training as laboratory assistants.

There is a subtler, human side to the internal *Where?* question. For the answer decides a man's neighbours, and much depends on that. If a room is situated close to a stores or a workshop, there will be little justification for the room containing sub-stocks of materials or machine tools—and for this reason, many scientists would choose to be far away from either! Of greater ultimate significance is the consequence that a man sees much more of his own near neighbours than of people separated by a block or even a staircase. Perhaps he ought to consult others, according to the constitution, but a sub-conscious aversion to even a short pilgrimage will mean that even slightly remoter sources are much less tapped. Moreover, there are many subjects which do not warrant being raised specifically, but which come in naturally in casual corridor conversation, so that an insidious influence can be built up undetected. Similar reasoning, of course, holds outside the laboratory walls, for contacts over a time-scale of months rather than days. This arises particularly when a laboratory attached to a large concern is intended to concentrate on fundamental research. Most people would agree that this is very difficult if the laboratory is under the same roof as a production department, since the clamour of production engineers for solutions to their short-term problems will side-track the research workers from their proper long-range tasks. Beware of the supposedly fundamental establishment that is not spatially remote. On the other hand, the remoteness need not be great. A journey of a mile will deter the busy productionist, while still allowing the scientist, in occasional slack times, to see what the real life is like at which his work must in the long run be aimed.

The local Where?

There is a small-scale aspect to the *Where?* question, that, whether they realise it or not, most research workers will face almost daily. Their work will be divided between library, office, laboratory, workshop, balance room, etc., and they will learn to apportion it. The framework may have been laid down more or less rigidly by the higher authorities—and these should be conscious of the consequences of their rulings—but there will be some spatial freedom left to the individual.

Some folk relish a glorious intermingling of all the activities that comprise their scientific life. At one and the same place (and very nearly one and the same time) they receive visitors, conduct experiments, write reports, construct apparatus, read abstruse books and store abstruse chemicals. No doubt this agrees with some temperaments and may be the means for their genius to bear fruit. While it may seem to give command of many activities at once, however, there is a grave risk that the day's programme will be decided, not by any rational plan, but by a series of random events, such as a beaker boiling over or a postman arriving with a journal that can be skimmed through.

We therefore suggest that for most people the more orderly approach is better. Escape to the fastness of the library to absorb the earlier scholarship in your subject. For the new experiment,

37

"Some folk relish a glorious intermingling of all the activities that comprise their scientific life"

clear a bench to receive the equipment whose intricacies have been fabricated elsewhere. And when baffled by the results, retire again to your desk so that you can review then dispassionately.

Although offices are most desirable to encourage objective thinking, they have their dangers. There is still an element of snobbery attached to the white-collar office-worker, and this will have a sub-conscious influence tending to make the man whose work should extend into both office and laboratory spend too long in the former. Even laboratories are not immune to conversation that is less technical than it might be, but the more intimate atmosphere of an office makes the danger greater there. A three-berth room is particularly susceptible: it is possible to refuse to converse oneself, but hardly to ban conversation by room-mates, so if any two occupants slip into a discussion of the test match or the inadequacy of salaries, the third will be condemned (unless blessed with mental ear-flaps) to abandon all work demanding serious reflection.

Old or new

When considering where he should work, the researcher may wonder whether he should choose an old laboratory or a new. The first answer may be that the new is obviously the more attractive: it was built in an age when science and its needs were (slightly!) better understood; it will incorporate modern accessories and luxuries; it will have adequate space for its inhabitants—though in fact laboratories have a curious knack of taking so long to build that they are overcrowded almost immediately they are occupied. The second answer may be to the effect that most of the best scientific work has been done in the structurally worst and oldest buildings. It would not be surprising if this were true. The creativity of a scientist is likely to be accompanied by an impatience that will not let him wait until a new building is available, but will make him devote his resources to essentials—assistants and apparatus in huts rather than a palace and a shortage of cash to back his latest brainchild. Moreover, the new buildings

39

may come as a reward for good work, which we will therefore expect to find correlated with the closing days of old accommodation. But we dare not recommend that, other things being equal, the older laboratory should be chosen. Rather should the entrant to the new premises beware that he is not obsessed with the idea of their newness. His choice of research topic and technique should not be unduly influenced by the new facilities at his disposal and his time should be given primarily and predominantly to his science rather than to praising and maintaining his housing. Similarly, of course, those in the old buildings must guard against a conservatism that engages in research that has become obsolete, merely because the establishment has equipment or a reputation for it.

Field experiments

We have discussed the importance of the laboratory. But in many cases, his laboratory will not be the only place where the scientist's research is conducted. 'Field experiments' is a wide phrase covering a wide range of activities, often significantly different from what is done in a laboratory.

Originally, no doubt, a field experiment was one in which the naturalist observed a nature fondly imagined to be uninfluenced by man—though why the world '*field*', presumably hedged, ploughed, manured and sown, should be used remains a mystery. The usage has been extended to cover investigations into systems that have been blatantly disturbed by man, in fact to cover anything that takes place remote from the laboratory. Whether the investigations concern Nature in the raw or human activities, they have much in common.

It is at first almost incredible to the laboratory-bound scientist how much less congenial field conditions are and how little conducive to calm scientific thought. Until we are really subject to them, we are apt to flatter ourselves that distracting circumstances will not impede our cool, collected meditation. I recall one field experiment, on naval communications, where the field was the sea. One experimenter sat calmly in a submarine below the reach of disturbing surface waves, finding great difficulty in appreciating the plight of his colleagues up above. The hope for link with them was never established, indeed the whole trip was largely unproductive, because the surface scientists could have little thought for anything but their own malaise and little hope of anything except that the wind would drop.

All possible thinking should be done in the home laboratory in advance of a field experiment. Experimental procedure should be planned in much greater detail than is normally justified for lab. work. Rehearsals should be conducted at the risk of tedium, so that actions become as mechanical as possible and so as to give such chance as may be for the unexpected catastrophe to declare itself. At the same time, when in the field a conscious effort must be made to act as calmly and deliberately as conditions allow.

Fields belong to people different from those who own laboratories. Placating the natives is always a most important issue in field work. The youthful and enthusiastic scientist is apt to forget that he is in a tiny minority, the world being very largely occupied by people to whom his reasoning is completely unintelligible; he learns at last how vain it is to expect that his rational, scientific arguments will carry the day. A co-operative attitude from the folk on the spot is desirable, often essential; but it is more easily found than fabricated. So, in selecting suitable sites for field work, this must be regarded as one of the highly relevant natural factors. If co-operation is to be produced or encouraged, it will be primarily by politeness and a readiness to see the other man's point of view. Remember that he is concerned with production—possibly even paid according to the quantity of it. Stop to think that a few disgruntled members of his staff—especially unjustifiably disgruntled ones—can poison relations over long periods. Spare some respect for the gentle conservatism which pays tribute to an honoured and often successful past. And if he has declared his interest in your work, remember to redeem your promise to send him a copy of the report you finally write.

While you respect the natives' position, this is not to say that you accept their suggestions as profitable. A scientifically design-ed experiment, which it should be second nature to a research worker to devise, is not a concept that comes at all readily to most people. The would-be helpful bystander is most likely to propose all sorts of exciting changes that might be introduced into the test aimed at elucidating the effect of a single, other variable.

On the other hand, the folk who have had to live with problems of Nature (or the inscrutability of some human artefacts) have often acquired a deep empirical wisdom about them. This could well provide a jumping off point for the researcher who has to tabulate, to analyse and to theorise. The difficulty, as in many another field, is one of communication, for the two parties do not speak a common language. The alert coal-face worker in a mine, for instance, knows a great deal about subterranean stress distri-bution; but none of the terms in which he describes it (and cer-tainly neither of the adjectives) will be used as defined in British Standards. So there is an acute problem of interpretation.

Field trials

If the field work is a field trial of apparatus that is planned to be used eventually in the field, further considerations apply. As early as possible in its development, the apparatus should be made rugged. Designers of war-time naval instruments reckoned that they should be AB-proof, an AB being a man who presumed that everything he touched was similar in strength to the battle-ship he lived on; that is a good standard to aim at. Unproved equipment should never be left to the tender mercies of a user who is not one of the laboratory's team: this does not mean that field tests should not be carried out—on the contrary—but that they should always be conducted by understanding and sympathetic personnel. Otherwise a malicious freak of Nature is sure to combine with a malicious streak of the operator and precipitate disaster.

Sometimes, the aim will be to insinuate a new instrument into a situation where the stalwarts of the past maintain that their existing gear is amply adequate and has been proved by a century of unmodified use. A frontal attack is then much less likely to effect an introduction than the approach under which permission is sought to try out the instrument from academic interest. When the new unit happens to be lying about, connected up, the old operators may, from curiosity, look at it and discover its utility before they have had occasion to think over all the arguments against it.

Visits

Constructive and original work is normally done in the laboratory or occasionally in the field, but it cannot be done in an intellectual vacuum, regardless of what is happening elsewhere. Therefore the scientist must sometimes leave the shelter of his own pastures to visit the world outside. Certainly there is need to keep a sense of perspective: if he is to keep himself thoroughly informed of all the investigations in other establishments that are relevant to his own, he will find that he has less than no time in which to do anything himself. But at least some minimum proportion of time must be spent on 'away' fixtures, learning what can be learnt from elsewhere. Some people will take excessive pleasure in being welcomed as visitors and will rank highly the honour of serving as something of an ambassador for their own concern. They will display keen interest in subjects that have nothing whatever to do with them, and feel that they are moving in exalted circles. Some will act as narrow specialists, dismissing as inadmissible every twist of conversation that is not a direct answer to questions of obvious common interest to host and visitor; they will take their departure as soon as a restricted agenda has been exhausted. But all must go visiting to a greater or less extent. They will do well to try to act in both capacities, going into the fullest detail of their own subject, and then seeking to widen their horizons as they imbibe the pet themes of their hosts.

When visiting—as, indeed, on most occasions—there is a

"They will display keen interest in subjects that have nothing whatever to do with them"

great advantage in being able to assess the other man soundly. For there will be some who will enthuse glibly over their own accomplishments, asserting that theirs is the only way to do it, adding perhaps that anyhow nothing is now left to be done— and all this on a very flimsy foundation of positive achievement. Some will be found, by contrast, who from humility or secrecy play down all that they have done. The skill to form a balanced judgment of both, to discount the former and to draw out the latter, is a great asset. It will go with the discernment of when to listen with silence or with supplementary questions and when to speak of personal experiences: as a rule, the visitor is to learn, the host to teach. (So we may look for the crossover point, whereafter calls received exceed calls paid, as giving an indication of scientific maturity!)

Conferences

On a more multilateral basis, of course, the visits will be to meetings and conferences. Every year, a longer list seems to be organised to tempt the traveller. Eyebrows at last are rising to query the previously axiomatic assumptions as to the worth-whileness of everything that is adequately patronised. Certainly it is dangerous to assume that because a jamboree was held in the last quinquennium a super-jamboree is essential for the next, and that if five hundred attended that one we must lure a thousand into coming to this. There is a severe danger of organisation for organisation's sake.

This difficulty is related to the delicate question of what level of specialisation the meeting is to be aimed at. At discussions where topics are dealt with in a general manner, there are only two reasons for attendance: firstly, for education, since many learners absorb their knowledge more readily from a good speaker than from the written word; and, secondly, in order that one's dutiful attendance should be noted, and if possible one's voice heard— the more general the subject, the more difficult it is for the chairman to prevent a contributor from riding his own irrelevant hobby horse. It behoves the organisers of meetings to encourage the former motivation and to discourage the latter.

When a more specialised subject is under consideration, there is an additional reason for being present. No doubt it is often possible to read the published proceedings, and thus to digest their content more thoroughly at leisure. But provided a reasonably lively discussion has ensued, the discerning listener will learn to get a feel for the general regard in which the subject matter is held. There may be an inkling of this in a published discussion, but it is unlikely that the edited version in cold print will convey quite the true shades of criticism or approbation. He that hath ears to hear, let him hear as well as read.

It is commonly agreed that the greatest value of conferences lies in the casual contacts they can bring about during coffee-breaks and the like. The organisers might consciously strive to make these easier, particularly trying to encourage the great and famous to meet the lowlier, more specialised workers: the combining of broad, general experience and detailed local knowledge on to a problem is a fruitful operation.

Interlingual communication

There is an obvious prize to be sought from international conferences by pooling experiences of a much larger number of scientists. A severe problem which immediately arises is that of translation. Of course, elaborate systems for simultaneous translation are now available, but any obstacles in the way of direct man-to-man communication reduce the advantages that a personal encounter has over a written communication. It would seem that this is not quite so important for a meeting between fellow-specialists: where two men have been working in closely similar fields, they will be aware of the basic difficulties that beset them both, and probably of the general alternative avenues of escape that present themselves. A single technical word serves to convey the vital information as to which route has been followed. Very likely, both parties will have adopted the same criteria by which to judge the effectiveness of a technique, and a single figure (which will be understood when written, if not when pronounced!) gives the measure of success achieved. In more general discussions, by contrast, the ideas to be communicated will often be subtler ones, where delicate shades of meaning have to be distinguished; the language barrier is then more severe, so much so that there would really seem little value in sitting through a lecture or discussion unless the hearer is well versed in the language of the original delivery. Of course, the benefit of continuing personal contact with an expert is quite independent of this. This may be an unpopular doctrine to promulgate in high places, since its corollary is that seniors should travel abroad less, and relative juniors more.

It is again elementary that if one wants to consider whether foreign ways could profitably be introduced at home, one must study them in their original surroundings. Equally if the other man's weaknesses and capabilities are to be appreciated, he must be seen on his home ground. Who, till he had travelled in it, would believe that the Dutchman's respect for age could reserve a lift to be operated only by those over thirty? Or who would understand the tidiness of the Germans as well as after finding in their front gardens notices addressed to the passing dogs and requesting them not to perform there as depicted in the drawing?

The average scientist, no less than the average anything else, enjoys foreign travel. He is, therefore, anxious to enjoy it as one of the perquisities in the course of his business. In the attempt to restrain this, authorities are often hard of persuasion about the need for the journey. The unfortunate sequel is that papers for conferences are often produced more as additional arguments to justify attendance than because there is any valuable information to put in them. With a resultant degrading of technical standards. Not only are foreign conferences enjoyable, but they also carry an implication of status. Expeditions (westward) across the Atlantic have particular weight, and those who have them to their credit soon learn the technique for leading the conversation to the point where they can quietly slip in the piece about their experience of the States.

47

Exhibitions

Exhibitions are a special subject for visiting, probably the most tiring of all. If they are to have value to the patron, he must stay alert. For, looking back, he will often find that while 95% of the exhibition was quite useless to him, the odd 5% gave him exciting, and often unexpected, information which he might well have missed if he had been more casual. One great advantage of an exhibition is the opportunity it provides for asking searching questions without compromising the questioner. Occasionally, academic staff will be present, to be engaged in conversations that might prove too brief to have justified a more formal approach. More often there will be a fair chance of finding the technical men of industry, unshielded by their Sales Departments; they can then be quizzed about their products, with no suggestion of an obligation to buy even if all the answers are satisfactory.

Remember to write up an account of your visit, wherever it is to, before the memory has faded. It is absurd to spend a day going and seeing, and then to grudge the extra hour, without which much of the visit's value will have been lost in a few short weeks.

Universality of thought

The scientist must, therefore, expect to work, not only in his own laboratory, but in other people's, in lecture theatres, in conference halls and in exhibition arcades. But the simple answer to the question: 'Where should he work?' is *'Everywhere'*. Research is something that must permeate a man's whole life if he is to do the best at it, not to the exclusion of all else, but as a background to it. Perhaps it is because it is an art. Perhaps this is what justifies science being called a profession. Perhaps all creative steps arise from the sub-conscious and the sub-controllable must be given freedom to throw up its ideas. Be those as they may, the scientist's laboratory actions will be feebler unless they are backed up by thoughts from the armchair, from the meditative walk or (like Archimedes) from the bath. Sometimes his mind will be casting back to old problems, sometimes it will be triggered by present events into new lines of thought. The Courtney-Pratt camera is said to have its origins in a Paris street, where there was a gadget in a shop window. This enabled every passer-by to see a succession of pictures of a young lady, the picture seen at any moment depending upon the angle from which the gadget was viewed. One passer-by did not think only of her different stages of deshabille but appreciated the potentialities of the idly used technique of image dissection*.

While the big questions concerning his research work must remain in a scientist's sub-conscious wherever he goes, we have urged that his interests in life should not by any means be restricted to these. It is a nice question whether his attitude to his 'extra-curricular' activities should be strictly scientific. One feels that, to the greatest men, a scientific approach will be so much second nature that they will be unable to shake it off whatever they are doing. For lesser mortals, contrasting diversion may be more justifiable. I can recall studying carefully in leisure hours the rate at which my bath cooled down—I think I found it impossible to equate it to a function of water temperature, air temperature and the depth as measured by the number of plug chain links immersed—but that was before I would have claimed to be a research worker. Nowadays, I take pride in cultivating my garden unscientifically.

---

* R. A. HAYES, High Speed Image Dissection Photography, *Industrial Image* (*Ilford*), 1 (1956) 3.

3. When?

A wise man's heart discerneth both time and judgment.   Eccles. 8:5.

In considering the apportioning of his time, the scientist will find that there are two scales on which it has to be done, the macroscopic—dealing with years—and the microscopic, concerned with days or even hours. Of course, the two shade into each other, and of course a year is made up of days, but we can conveniently think of the two aspects separately.

Planning a career

We are not sufficiently masters of our fate to have any confidence that detailed planning of our career will be realised. That is no justification for refusing to give any thought to the subject. The scientific approach—or perhaps this is more a matter of engineering—is to make plans which extend far ahead but take firmer shape as the date for their fulfilment approaches, and which are subject to revision in the light of experience.

Someone whom I cannot recall resolved to divide his life into three equal periods of twenty-five years each. The first was to be spent training, the second earning his living and making his name, and the third enjoying the fruits of the second. When writing his auto-biography in retirement, the campaign was proceeding according to plan. But I believe he was not a scientist—more likely a barrister. The research worker is likely to find that the phases merge into one another. His formal training will end abruptly, but he would be unwise to regard himself as omniscient

50

thereafter. He should also find that the enjoyment is largely blended with both the other stages—fortunately, since it would be very rash to count on a full twenty-five years after they are ended.

Compared with other professions, only a very small minority of scientists are their own masters. To some people, this will appear a distinct drawback; if such have a compulsion to research, they should join university staffs, where a man at least has leasehold rights in his own time, even if he is not the ground landlord. With the aim of greater independence, a more general corollary is that a research worker may find it wise to seize what opportunities do present themselves to add to his career such sidelines and diversions as may prevent him from being a too rigidly bound 9 to 5.30 employee.

Diversity of scientists' concerns

In fact, a considerable element of opportunism goes well with a laboratory career. There is so much else that is incidentally involved in the work, besides manipulating test-tubes or evaluating formulae. The man from the lab. may later have to mix with the man from the factory, when he will keep his end up better if he has first-hand experience of real life in a factory. He will be sure to encounter manual skills and the need to appraise them, which he will scarcely find possible if he has never laboured to acquire any himself. Above all, he will meet people of all sorts, the long and the short and the tall, in both physical and mental stature. Again and again he will have the need to assess them, and for this he cannot have too much experience. So he should take any opportunity, especially in his younger days when dignity will deny it less sternly, to gain experience in other walks of life. One specific example is teaching. During the earlier years of research, when a man is beginning to realise, and perhaps to remedy the depth of his ignorance, it may seem a waste of time to pile on the labour of part-time teaching; although he might find any extra remuneration helpful. But later in life, perhaps moving nearer towards whole-time teaching, perhaps advising on education and careers, previous experience of the discipline of even a junior-class blackboard could be invaluable.

How far to take formal education

One of the things outside his laboratory that he should follow after is further education. There are many things to be learned. But there is a risk of going too far. It is true that, for most of us, natural lethargy and conservatism will provide a powerful brake against initiative. For some people, however, there is a real danger of attempting too much, especially at the junior academic levels. Most men who have watched the progress of laboratory staff over a few years could give examples of those who have set themselves a target—perhaps of an external degree—and have toiled on in pursuit of this for much too long. Probably force of habit kept them at it, rather than a rational decision. The end may have been a final, disillusioned abandonment of their quest. Little less unfortunate, it may have been a nominal achievement of success, but one that has left them with little energy or initiative, conditioned to learn orthodox things from the book rather than to blossom with original proposals.

There is no simple way out of the dilemma. The studious young scientist must acquire that most difficult knowledge, knowledge of himself, and assess his own capabilities. He must make due allowance for his wife's ambitions or love of ease (which will be liable to affect both the assessment and the capability). Then he must set his course, aiming at some academic target, and remembering to review the situation periodically but not continuously. The review is likely to be the more agonising because of the separateness of courses at different levels, which generally makes it necessary to start again distressingly near the beginning after altering the aim either upwards or downwards (let alone sideways).

We believe, then, that the young scientist, as he starts his career, should look about him to see how he can broaden his interests and widen his experience. He should also, in consciousness of his own limitations, continue his academic progress to a reasonable height. This latter will include, for most scientific disciplines, reaching appropriate standing in his institute or institution. These bodies generally play a large enough part in the life of the profession for it to be a handicap to ignore them; whether it is every member's role to become well-known by featuring prominently in their activities is another matter, calling again for a measure of conscious thought and deliberate decision. These things should all be decided in the light of the master-plan, so far as it has been worked out, for the individual's whole career. To the latter he must give most earnest attention, debating what situation he really wants to have reached at what age; it is certainly sensible to aim at leaving several options open as long as possible, but it is equally certainly foolish to have no thinking and planning directed beyond the immediate future. The wise man will look ahead, at least occasionally, right up to his retirement. Dare we point out the apparent disproportion often encountered in the meticulous attention given to every stage up to and including the leisure years of retirement by those who resolutely refuse to admit any consideration of subsequent events?

How long in one post?

Everyone has to decide when to move from one post to another. Topical happenings may, of course, play a large part or precipitate events, but decisions are better made against an objective background. Cases will vary widely, but we would suggest that the experience which a scientist gains from doing one particular job shows diminishing returns as indicated in Fig. 5, with perhaps something of a knee at the 5-year mark. This is not by any means to say that every enterprising research worker will be searching diligently for a fresh employer before those five years are up. For one thing, he may get a different job from the same employer.

More important is the realisation that experience gained is only part of the story. There is giving as well as getting, and even from

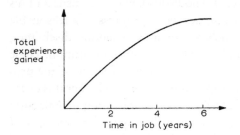

Fig. 5. Experience gained in one job.

a selfish point of view the scientist must remember that his assets include the research work he has accomplished as well as the configuration of the storage cells in his brain. If we plot research output against the time in one job, we may get Fig. 6. For a junior role, the time lag T_l may be measured only in weeks, but if the individual concerned is standing on his own feet, making a

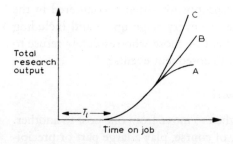

Fig. 6. Research output from one job.

substantial contribution to knowledge, it is likely to be two or three years. There will be new technical situations to size up, a case history to appraise, fresh tools, both administrative and material, to learn to handle and new colleagues to get to know; and none of this can be hurried. Most Ph. D. students would testify to the way in which almost no research has been done until almost all their grant has run out.

The later part of the output–time curve is highly dependent on the particular job tackled. It may flatten off again, at least temporarily, after a limited objective has been reached (A). It may continue upwards with a fairly steady slope (B). It may even, by a fortunate combination of person and project, steepen in its climb (C). These are the matters to consider, in conjunction with the fresh experience that may be gained, when debating whether to move. On the whole, more weight should be attached to widening experience in the earlier years, and scientists—and their employers—should guard against becoming too engrossed in narrow specialities. After sampling the delights of one or two fields of work, it may be wise to settle down for longer at one attractive subject and to concentrate on achieving a smooth flow of research results.

In any plans—about when to do what—that reach further ahead, one of the most important variables to be taken into account is the planner himself. We have sketched in Figs. 7, 8 and 9 some of the parameters by which he can be described. There is, of course, an enormous spread between individuals, even where we have not indicated this; the curves refer to the hypothetical *Average Scientist*. 'Know Yourself' questionnaires have had their vogue, and it would be an interesting exercise for the career planner to plot the particular curves that he expects to apply to himself: his wife might be able to furnish him with figures for the present values and perhaps also the present slopes (though some skill might be needed to choose times for sampling that would give statistically significant answers).

Scientist or administrator

However, be those things as they may, there is need to give close attention to how later years will be spent. Some entrants to the research industry will be clear that they intend to be researchers all their lives; their ambition is scientific rather than social. There

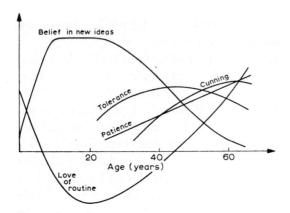

Fig. 7. Character shift with age.

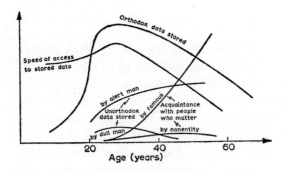

Fig. 8. Memory at different ages.

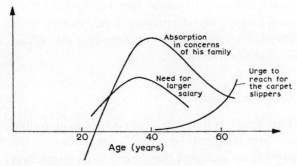

Fig. 9. Home influence at different ages.

56

should always be a welcome for them. The one anxiety should be to ensure that they are in lines of research that will persist throughout their working lives; increasing care must be bestowed on the choice of subject as increasing age makes any changes increasingly difficult.

Some entrants will have an equally clear intention to climb steadily to the top of their administrative tree. The route thither is tolerably clear, though they will sometimes have difficult decisions. The choice between changing their subject often to gain wide experience for administration and specialising to achieve fame is a delicate one. Similarly, it is a tricky assessment to balance the immediate gains from grasping at every promotion that offers itself against the risk of being thought unstable. The young climbers, however, must be warned not to judge their own prospects by the present situation. The explosion of population in the research world that has occurred over a few decades has strongly favoured those who started out a generation ago; there have been relatively very few people available for the senior positions. The recent numerical growth of research workers cannot continue exponentially, or there will be nobody left in industry to make the profits and pay the taxes on which research must feed. As the steady state is approached, there is bound to be proportionately less room at the top. (Will this mean that, with more to select from, we can expect higher quality in the direction of our research, or is the cream already available, so that the extra queue for the director's chair will be largely composed of second-rate material?) Even apart from the changing overall situation, it must be recognised that only a small minority of working scientists are destined to reach positions of wide responsibility. I hope that any emphasis here on the ambitious organising of a career will not be taken as an unsettling implication of unrealistic prospects.

In between those anxiously determined to reach the heights and those simply bent on a lifetime at the laboratory bench, come the majority without a very clearcut idea of where they will travel. They may hope for wider responsibility without the agony of bitter disappointment if it should pass them by. These, as we have counselled, should consider their careers from year to year, examining any direction that may accord with the developing technical situation and with their own developing inclinations and abilities. Especially in view of the limited number of openings in senior positions and of the frustrations in simple research in old age for all but the very dedicated, we would urge that increasing attention should be paid to research workers moving out from their laboratories to other useful activities. A background of research is useful in many occupations, and is going to be increasingly so, as the pace of technological change quickens and innovations come to succeed each other with no pause for operators to be familiarised. No hint of stigma should be attached to a move from research in middle life; the scientists left behind should rather think of their colleague as an emissary who has gone to civilise the benighted natives in other walks of life. As we have indicated, the possibility of such moves later should provide an incentive for gaining appropriate wider experience as opportunities arise at earlier stages of a career.

The stages of a discovery

Let us turn now to the more microscopic aspect of *When?*, considering the day-to-day, or perhaps more accurately the week-to-week arrangement of the researcher's time. His work is essentially concerned with the making of discoveries; this must be continually in mind, to prevent the risk of being side-tracked up side-alleys. As a background to deciding the apportionment of time, we may try to analyse the course of a discovery, breaking it down into stages. A discovery begins with the query whether that particular hypothesis could be true—this holds even for a novel observation made out of the blue, for the cautious observer's first reaction will always be to wonder if he can trust his apparatus or his senses. As the discovery proceeds, the query becomes a possibility which grows into a probability and finally emerges as certainty, or as near to certainty as it is decent to approach in science. This is not the end of the business, for it still remains to tell the world about it.

There is often a tendency to lay most emphasis on the stage of growing probability, which can easily be seen to offer scope for dramatic incidents. But in fact the first and last parts of the incident are often of the greatest importance. Firstly, it is always essential to ask the right questions; people have been fobbed off too readily with the comment that fools can ask questions which the learned cannot answer—those questions are generally not worth answering anyhow. It takes a wise man to ask a wise question. And in research, the scientist must continually be debating whether he is tackling the right question, for those who are good at answers seldom contribute as much as those who are good at questions. In a large establishment, the newcomer will generally find that his problems have been formulated for him— this is the chief justification for having another scientist in charge of him—but he should be alert to appraise the situation and even, very tactfully, to point it out if he is convinced that he is answering unprofitable questions.

The last stage is also more important than the newcomer often realises. A scientific discovery, or a technological development, should be thought of, not as an isolated incident, but as part of a world-wide growth of ideas and abilities. From that point of view, linking in to other growing points is an essential feature of the operation. Even when he is working for a single firm, whom he may fondly imagine to be waiting with bated breath for the outpouring from his laboratory, the developer will all too often find that much the hardest part of his work is convincing potential users of the significance and value of what he has done. Britain is perhaps notorious and unique in this respect.

Writing up

It follows that when a campaign is being planned, careful attention must be paid to the desirability of writing up what has been achieved at different stages. There is a great satisfaction in dealing with a subject exhaustively before it is released for publication: Roentgen is said to have investigated X-rays so thoroughly, before announcing his discovery of them, that there was nothing left for other physicists to do about them for several years after*. There is a risk in this that he who really made the discovery may appear to be anticipated. There is a greater danger, for the applied scientist, that the unpublished work will have a reduced relevance with the passage of time. Lord Hinton talks of the *'moving target'* that research is aimed at, pointing out that if the answers come too late, technology will have moved on and the original questioners will have evaded the need for having the answers.

But there are very different degrees of writing up. The first solution to reconciling the rival claims of taciturnity and verbosity is to write freely for restricted circulation and sparsely for broadcast distribution. The occasional comprehensive paper will be much more easily compiled if it has been preceded by several local notes dealing with particular aspects of it. These can cover even quite small stages in the progress of the work; certainly for many complicated experimental set-ups, the correct functioning of the apparatus is a milestone well worth celebrating in ink. Moreover, the devious machinations by which it was achieved will then be much more clearly in mind; later, unless the ill-wind of frequently needed repetition has blown, all the processes of adjustment and all the accessories introduced may have drifted peacefully out of memory. The human memory, in fact, is basically a sensationalist**. It will recall extremes in either direction, but when a reading is an indifferent one, which by itself neither proves nor disproves the point at issue, memory will be apt to prove most misleading. So, write down promptly.

There is a continual battle of self-discipline to be fought concerning writing. Possibly the more pedestrian researcher is quite

---

* P. P. EWALD, William Henry Bragg and the New Crystallography, *Nature*, 195 (1962) 320.

**P. FREEDMAN, *The Principles of Scientific Research*, Macdonald, London, 1949, p. 156.

content to escape the searing creativity of new thoughts by conscientiously chronicling what has happened. The more eager and restless souls who are impatient to make great discoveries (and are the essential ingredients if a laboratory is to be alive) will find that they tend to draw their conclusions only from the salient facts of what has happened and to press on with the next move. But they too must stop to write.

Often it will be found helpful just to sit down at the stage the research happens to have reached, and to put the current arguments in writing. A sheet of paper is not quite such a good foil to the reasoning powers as is an intelligent and well-versed colleague, but it is generally more readily obtainable—and it does keep to the point better. Such a documented and dated soliloquy will often settle later points of dispute as to what state the art had reached when, as well as making much clearer which of several possible next moves should immediately be taken.

The answer to the question: "*When write?*" is thus nearly always: "More often than you want to".

One of the advantages of writing up adequately the work that has already been achieved is that it provides an opportunity for thinking whether that particular field of study has really been exhausted. Until an argument is down on paper, it will nearly always seem obvious that more remains to be done—a detail filled in, a more convincing proof of some questionable point, a repetition with alternative material. And often, it would really be more profitable to accept that the seam is almost worked out, that the law of diminishing returns is strongly applicable, and that a new start should be made with a radically new investigation. Certainly, these decisions concerning new beginnings are about the most important that a scientist has to make: it is a good thing that several heads are commonly put together to think the matter out. Some people, of course, are temperamentally suited for the hard plodding that is involved in piling up results of a repetitive nature; some, moreover, will be inclined to flit too light-heartedly from one topic to another as their fancy happens to be seized. But, on the whole most will want shaking up and pushing into

"He is constrained to hammer away at his problem, regardless of times and conventions"

new subjects half against their will. There may be some advantage in one man, if he has the breadth of mind, retaining an interest in two lines of work, one of which is a semi-routine exploitation of a previous innovation, while the other involves breaking radically new ground elsewhere. But he will need a good lieutenant to support him.

Variable pace of research

It will normally be found that, over the years, there is a wide variety in the pace of research work. Sometimes it will seem that for months at a stretch very little happens. Perhaps there is a long wait for items of equipment from elsewhere; perhaps just a multiplicity of minor delays and frustrations so that it is hard to account for the time that has passed fruitlessly. While that phase is on, a large measure of patience is demanded. This must not develop into too ready an acceptance of time frittered away. Some sense of inspiration must be maintained, and as we have suggested before, a second line of activity for the research worker can be very useful here, be it only taking a live interest, at second-hand, in the technical subjects that only border on his own prime concern.

Interspersed with these sterile periods will come sessions (an inappropriate word, if it is derived from something to do with sitting down) of much greater activity. Sometimes these will be imposed from outside: a date must be met, either for a dated exhibition or for a field trial that is woven in with some unchangeable programme. Sometimes they will arise simply from the working of a creative mind. It does happen on occasion that an idea comes tumbling out, carrying with it the urge to test it, and the repercussions and the conquences build up to demand immediate investigation; energy and enthusiasm to match the occasion surge into the thinker and he is constrained to hammer away at his problem, regardless of times and conventions. For the great majority, these will be rare—all too rare—occasions. It will be well to pander to the mood, and to foster its enthusiasm.

63

While it is unwise to inject an excess of artificial drama into the situation, it may well be sound to emphasise anything which can encourage a note of urgency, insisting for instance on adhering more closely to a target timetable than might seem warranted by an unemotional appraisal of the facts.

Such a panic pursuit of a newly sighted scientific objective must not be allowed to degenerate into a completely blind chase. There is a risk that an attachment to the original idea will become so obsessive that it will be followed even after the first results have shown that the position hoped for is untenable. Sometimes it will be desirable to sleep on it so that the cold light of morning can bring the visionary face to face with realities.

Another danger of the spasmodic mode of life is that it inveigles the liver into overestimating how hard he is working. The memory of his all-night session will continue with him long after he has forgotten the half-holidays that he took to make up for it and because the work was temporarily in the doldrums. Beware of irregular hours, observing them with scientific accuracy and unbiassed sampling. When you are on overtime, agree that it is right and natural for the length of a scientist's working day to fluctuate wildly; but when tempted to short hours, keep the ideal of a routine timetable steadily in front of you.

It cannot be emphasised too strongly that the exciting phase of research, when results tumble over themselves to be found, is all too rare. Sad disillusion awaits the man who expects such satisfaction without the long, hard grind of preparation. Particularly is this so when entering a new field of study. An extensive background must be absorbed before there is a hope of being able to assess critically the ideas which come to mind—or even to judge which part of the field is ripest for investigation. There is a tale of two company directors, who, fired with enthusiasm for this new thing, *Research*, that everyone spoke well of, engaged a Scientist. He duly started work one day, and at 11 a.m. the Chairman said to the Managing Director: "Shall we see if he has invented something?" "No", said the M.D., "We mustn't rush him; we'd better wait till lunch".

64

Secondary interests

So the times of inspiration and intense activity need fostering and
making the most of. They must not, however, be exaggerated so
that everything else is regarded as killing time until they come.
A great deal of excellent research has been done without fever-
heat ever being reached, and it is essential to have the self-discipline to continue working away at a subject even when the
incentive of anticipated quick returns is missing. It is also wise to
think out how and when to fit in the secondary interest that we
have suggested is often a sound accompaniment to a research
career. If this is teaching, the lecturing times will be inescapably
set, but not the time for preparation. If it is preparing abstracts
or giving general advice, the clamour of the customer will have
some regulating action, but it will be well to anticipate this in
some measure with a prepared plan. If the secondary interest is
writing books, experience has taught that the provision of adequate time is an almost insoluble problem; perhaps the best
answer would be to be sent to prison for a month every year or so.

Diaries

The young scientist may smile at finding the extent to which men
are slaves to their diaries; they dare not commit themselves to do
anything without first asking the permission of the taskmaster. It
is only later in life that this tyranny takes on its more extreme
form, but it is well to learn early of its dangers. For it is strange
how easily that most precious commodity, time, can be allocated,
not according to some carefully thought out master-plan, but in
a random manner decided merely by the bookings in the diary. It
is commonly too easily conceded that any person or cause has a
right to claim the next vacant page in the diary. The vicious
consequence of this is that those things—such as general reading
or casual talking—which are never entered in the diary tend to
get squeezed out of the life of the busy man without his making
any conscious decision to that end. In the extreme case, not only
the unentered items are lost, but also many appointments that the

65

busy man should initiate, and which get squeezed out by arrangements made by his colleagues or the administrative machine. Some will resolutely refuse to be hamstrung by routine, ignoring it—regardless of the chaos that ensues—when the mood takes them. Others will find the only solution to lie in deliberately setting aside sabbatical days, on which no ordinary business may be transacted.

Reading

An important secondary occupation is just reading. Sometimes, of course, it is a primary occupation—when the research has reached a stage at which it is essential to survey what similar things have been done elsewhere, or when another person's technique is to be employed and so needs studying. As a primary occupation, reading tends to look after itself, though each individual might analyse himself, as to whether he is the receptive type who will read too much or the active type who will read too little, and add appropriate correction factors to his tendencies.

The more thorny problem is the continual, general contact that must be maintained with technical literature over the years. There will be a temptation to skimp this, since the time so saved can give a short-term increase in output. But this should surely be held as very much of an emergency reserve, only to be broken into in really dire straits. Otherwise there will be a progressive loss in familiarity with the strides the rest of the world has made and a corresponding reduction in the scientist's potential value. There are two objectives of such reading. The localised aim is to ensure that no developments relevant to the current work are overlooked. With this in mind, not only should direct rivals be watched for, but also the discoveries made in neighbouring fields: they may suggest analogies for a theory, or supply missing constants for an equation. Similarly, instruments or techniques developed for a different customer might well be adapted to serve the ends of the alert reader. The wider purpose of week-to-week reading is to stay informed about developments elsewhere that,

66

in the long run, might have repercussions in other fields. The relative proportions of what falls in the two categories will vary with seniority—over an almost infinite range: it might be taken as an index of managerial responsibility or at least of the responsibility which the reader thinks himself to have.

Even though the problem of finding time is a formidable one, this loosely directed reading must not be cut out, nor even, very far, be cut down: some organisations have firmly recommended that 20% of working time be spent reading*. Various abstracting services are available with the laudable aim of streamlining the absorption of the literature. This is probably admissible for our first category. Any closely relevant papers will then be called for for a study of the original, and a reference card should be made out— as well as facilitating future searches, the reference card has a psychological effect by giving a stronger impression that something positive has been achieved from time spent. It is doubtful if abstracts have so much value for the more general reading: part of the aim of this is to gain the sort of feeling for the state of a subject that can come from skimming through an article but hardly from reading another man's summary of the situation. And if no-one thumbs idly through the journals, the advertisers will come to realise that it is not worth buying space, and the price of the journals will go up!

Detailed programme planning

The central time problem, however, is not the organisation of peripheral activities, but the planning of a research programme. Unfortunately, this is almost impossible to do. A research that is approaching the limits of what can be achieved by the experimental techniques currently available is likely to be baulked repeatedly by malfunctioning of apparatus. An investigation that

---

* "The Use of Technical Literature by Industrial Technologists", *Social Survey Report No.* 245, Central Office of Information, 1959. Discussed *J. Inst. Elec. Engrs. (London)*, 5 (1959) 687.

poses a fundamental question will have its sequel decided by the answer to that question. It might almost be said (and it would receive some support from information theory) that predictability is an index of triviality. Nevertheless, it is very desirable, to the extent that it is possible—which may be very limited—to plan ahead. This is primarily to clear the thinking of the planner. If he has to set down which of two matters he will deal with first, he will be compelled to weigh their relative importance. If he makes the effort to draw up a timetable, he may be forced to realise that one cherished development can only come to fruition too late to have any value for the main work. Therefore a realistic appraisal of programmes and time-scales for research is no more to be scoffed at than a realistic marshalling of scientific evidence.

As in many fields, the many-body problem is much the more complicated. It it is desirable for an individual to work out what he, one man, should do, and when, it is essential to go through this exercise when a number of parties, with inter-locking schedules and concerns, are involved. Perhaps it will be helpful to chart the different stages against the dates when they should be completed: often this seems trivial, but the human mind seems to take in diagrammatic representations easily. If there is not to be a danger of their misleading, such charts should actually be compiled by the person for whose information they are intended. This will ensure that he understands the meaning of the different sub-divisions into which the project has been broken down; otherwise, so much explanatory detail will be needed that the chart loses its simplicity and its point.

The programmer will find that some of the actions he has scheduled fall to himself, while some are the responsibility of other people at different degrees of remoteness. Let him remember the difficulties arising from the inertia of other people, and—while not neglecting to apply a large force to that large inertia—to plan his timetables around them. In particular, he should always carry out first those of his own tasks that will enable his colleagues to get started on theirs. His flexibility (to alter the mechanical analogue) will then offset their rigidity; his output will increase because he will be more likely to have more people working for him.

One benefit conferred by the written programme, composed as the researcher meditates over his tasks, is that it will list the low priority work as well. Sometimes this will never get done as such: it will either become unnecessary or increase in priority. But sometimes the main lines of attack will all be held up awaiting some hardware or some decision, and time will hang more heavily. The second-line activities we have discussed—of teaching, administration, etc.—may then occupy attention, but often it will prove more suitable to clear off some of the minor jobs which were set down at the last assessment as interesting but not essential.

It is especially important to have such 'jobs for rainy days' when there are juniors in the laboratory. Secondary interests they cultivate for themselves may be highly irrelevant to the advancement of science, and there is a greater danger for them of being held up while the thinking is done in more exalted places; while the danger of reduced morale from under-employment is always acute. Therefore standing orders should always include an adequate list of tasks to be undertaken whenever more pressing occupations run out.

Daily timetables

We have dealt with—or at least flirted with—the macroscopic and the microscopic answers to 'When?' We conclude with a few considerations on the sub-microscopic scale—that of fractions of a day.

How should a scientist order his day? No doubt, the answers, even the right answers, can range from one incompatible extreme to the other. Nearly all would recognise the fact that when the human brain is applied to a fresh task of any moment there is a long induction period before full productivity is reached. Therefore, the timetable should be devised to allow relatively long uninterrupted spells when really significant work is being at-

"*Secondary interests juniors cultivate for themselves may be highly irrelevant to the advancement of science*"

tempted; possibly this may sometimes demand an appearance of surliness in relation to the orthodox social occasions such as tea-drinking. But, important though they are, these periods of concentration should be expected to be the exception rather than the rule: most people need diversion and relief from the commoner everyday tasks. At one stage of my career, having providently equipped myself with a pair of scissors, I found I was lending them to a junior from the library much more frequently than using them myself; but my generous offer that he could keep them in the library for the time-being was firmly declined on the grounds that that would deprive him of his only excuse for escaping from incarceration.

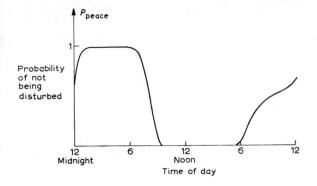

Fig. 10. Prospects of undisturbed work at different times of day.

So the common sequence for many scientists will be long periods of rather ordinary work interspersed with occasional spells of much more intense activity. This may be helped by careful planning of a 24-hour day, but individuals will vary enormously as to which plan is appropriate for them. Most thoughtful people would testify to the greatly enhanced value of the hour at the office when no-one else is about. Some would say it should be before the others have arrived; some might go further and maintain that the dawn hours are so productive that they should not be wasted on an employer! Others would take a

"An appearance of surliness in relation to the orthodox social occasions such as tea-drinking"

72

precisely opposite view. I have heard one learned gentleman quoted as saying: "Nine o'clock is all very well as a time for dustmen and milkmen, but for scientists—no" while the Rev. Frank Ballard remarked on the providence with which the good Lord had planned that normally only those who loved us best should see us before breakfast. In Fig. 10 we have indicated the prospects of undisturbed work at different hours. Whether or not that particular shape is valid for any individual, he could profitably construct his own P_{peace} curve and order his daily routine in the light of it.

Sleep

Unfortunately, action and reaction are often equal and opposite in the affairs of men as well as machines, and many people will

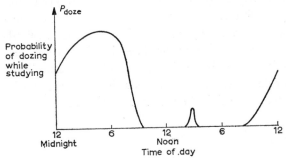

Fig. 11. Probability of dozing while studying at different times of day.

find a Fig. 11 applying to them to frustrate a good deal of the potentialities of Fig. 10. For your comfort, you may observe that we have indicated no scale for P_{doze}. The graph could perhaps be made much more widely applicable if the ordinate were some normalized quantity containing the total daily percentage of sleep raised to a high negative power.

More immediately applicable, we would urge that the minor, post-prandial peak in Fig. 11 should not be ignored. Planning, by those subject to this peak, should definitely aim at that hour for stimulating activities, since it has been established* that even a serious loss of sleep impairs performance only at uninteresting subjects, and not at those with sufficient fascination. For many men do seem to have a strong second harmonic component added to their fundamental daily rhythm. It may be that the Churchillian technique of sleeping in two instalments would prove the most satisfactory answer, but most of us will have to climb much farther towards being our own masters before we can escape from the straitjacket of convention into such radical solutions.

It is tempting to try to parallel the graphs of Fig. 7 with ones on a time-scale of hours to show the cyclic daily variations. But in truth there is such a wide spread between individuals that the whole of the available area would be shaded in to cover different cases. As we have indicated, an individual should consider carefully his own characteristic curves and order his day accordingly. He may find he needs a simple routine for the first half-hour until his brain has got adjusted to the shock of being at work; alternatively, he may find that the soporific influence of his surroundings is such that it will only be during the early minutes, before it has exerted its full force, that he is capable of creative thought! Of course, if the daily timetable cannot be adjusted, there may be nothing for it but to modify the characteristic curves.

Overtime

Note that the reward for an extra hour's work in a day is not necessarily just commensurate with the proportion of one in, say, eight. For, in one sense, the eight are already bespoke on the ordinary matters which a man owes for his living. It is the extra that allows him to venture into the original, to anticipate the opposition's manoeuvre, or to become devastatingly familiar with his own subject. But do not be misled into thinking that hard work alone is enough; if he is really to make his mark, the

---

* R. T. WILKINSON, Do We Sleep Too Much?, *New Scientist*, (5th May 1960) 1122–1123.

scientist must build on a native wit that will be very difficult to grow if he has not been born and bred with it. Granted that wit, then output will be more than proportional to the time spent outputting.

From what we have said, it may be remarked that much of the struggle to order our days seems to consist of a battle with sleep. It is curious that so little is known of the limits bounding what we can do with sleep—and what we can do without. There is considerable scope for investigating this further. It might enable us to reclaim an unsuspected volume of time: the malicious question as to what the skimping, scraping and reclaiming is all ultimately aimed at obviously belongs in another chapter.

4. Who?

Who knoweth the interpretation of a thing?
Eccles. 8:1.

School influence

An incredible number of ostensibly independent variables have combined, gentle reader, to fashion you. The science of the disentanglement of features caused by heredity and early environment has not yet proceeded very far, but for studying the adult scientist we can lump together most of the influences from his schooldays and earlier. Of the complex factors which predispose a youngster to choose one career or another, there can be little doubt that example ranks high, even though the choice is thought to have been made impersonally. Schoolteachers therefore carry a double weight of responsibility: not only must they liven the subject they teach, as a subject, but also they have the severe task of forming illustrations of the sort of people its proponents may grow to be*.

It is thus of primary importance that our schools should be staffed with enthusiasts who plead for science—the more so since there is necessarily competition for schoolchildren's allegiance. The pupils of one generation are the teachers of the next, so there is a circle—vicious or virtuous. The danger of perpetuating a tragic state of affairs does not seem fully realised, nor the extent to which the dice are already loaded against science

---

* Sir EDWARD APPLETON, Shortage of Science Applicants to Universities, *Nature*, 205 (1965) 232–233.
GARETH JONES AND DONALD HUTCHINGS, Sixth Formers' Attitudes to Technology, *New Scientist*, 17 (1963) 239–242.

at the schools. For the teacher of arts subjects could find few other places where his work would be so directly concerned with his own subject; if he is partial to the humanities—the subjects concerned with human beings—his very teaching as well as what is taught, will be heavily involved in them. Therefore, there will be a tendency for those keenest for their subject to be attracted to a school career. But with the sciences, it is different. We can hardly say that there is competition from industry: the teaching profession is almost a non-starter, if there is thought to be a race to beguile scientists into different walks of life. Cash and kudos are both much less at school. Especially would we emphasise the prestige value that has fastened on to research, making him a very dedicated man who defies it in order to guide youthful feet soundly into the paths of science. The opportunities provided in recent years, for schoolmasters to undertake research*, could make a useful, if small contribution. All this adds up to the distressing probability of a dearth of first-rate scientific personnel in the ranks of the schoolteachers, making not only for bad teaching but for a bad impression given of scientists: statistics of vacancies bear this out, and emphasise how particularly vicious is the circle in girls' education.

We might, therefore, ask rather anxiously whether the distribution of pupils between *Arts* and *Science* is made aright. Even the numerical proportion is not now moving so clearly in favour of Science; the maldistribution of quality may be even more dangerous. It is popularly supposed that children interested in things and in precisely expressed ideas will opt for Science, while those concerned with people and with less exact ideas will go Arts. That is all right as far as it goes, though the successful scientist will have a lot of delicate dealings with his fellow-men, and we may be in for trouble if our man-handling Arts people can't get their ideas exact enough. It may be wondered whether such a division is fundamental or whether it is a matter of chance (or teacher inspiration) which way the interests turn.

---

* *Nature*, 205 (1965) 235.

Perhaps there is a common quality factor. We discuss a little later the subject of creativity. Most professions are crying out for it, for people who can produce new and valid ideas, and those fields will flourish which can gain the larger share of such people. Most who consider the problem would agree that this country is so dependent on science and technology that it is economically important that these subjects should receive a generous share of the creativity available—though we would not dismiss lightly the argument that the world's technological competence has out-run its feeling for beauty and its moral sense, and that the balance needs redressing. Thinking along these lines, a note has recently been published* which starts to open up interesting possibilities. A tentative attempt was made to distinguish creative ability from 'ordinary' intelligence, and it was found that the ratio of the former to the latter was significantly greater for sixth-formers studying History than for their schoolfellows doing Physical Science. Various explanations of the results could be put forward, but if a lack of creativity should be substantiated it would bode ill for the future of research.

A further predisposition for which schools should probably share the blame, is the preference shown by most of the ablest youngsters for pure science rather than engineering. A many-sided campaign is needed to redress this balance. Have the possiblilities been fully explored of calling some of the material studied at school 'engineering'? I remember, when I got to college, wondering where all the chaps there called engineers had come from, since no subject like that had featured in my school curriculum; others, nowadays, may not be so naive, but I think a lot is still needed to bring home the exciting possiblilities of new subjects at an early stage.

---

* L. Hudson, Intelligence, Divergence and Potential Originality, *Nature*, 196 (1962) 601–602.

As we think *Who* the research workers are, then, we find that some of their characteristics have been shaped in them by school-leaving time. A further deposit is added at college. We are assuming, you will note, that all scientists have been to college. There is, admittedly, a sizeable minority who have come up the harder way, studying only part-time. At present, they include a few exceptional and invaluable characters among some indifferent ones. Their recruitment, however, is shrinking, as the educational machine becomes more ruthlessly efficient, and some who would have tended towards this route are now effectively catered for by sandwich courses.

A great deal of study is, of course, at present being given to the matter of university curricula, and this is not the place to expatiate thereon at length. The basic problem appears to be that of simultaneously accommodating two different requirements—the imparting of factual knowledge and the teaching to think. The former tends to receive much the greater emphasis, perhaps because it is more easily subjected to ordeal by examination, but the latter, for the creative scientists on whom a research laboratory essentially depends, is the more important. This is not to deny that a certain basic foundation of knowledge is needed: otherwise far too much time will be wasted speculating up blind alleys and consulting other authorities. Nor is it to hide the fact that there will be many in a laboratory of very limited creative capabilities, whose contribution—not to be despised —will therefore depend on their producing and applying slickly the facts and opinions that others have garnered. But if the cramming in of facts is undertaken so vigorously that it extinguishes the light of original thought, then higher—at least, the highest—education will have failed.

This is a danger that will grow. As the frontiers of knowledge are pushed further out, so the trails to reach them must grow longer, and the pioneers who are to extend them still further will be increasingly exhausted by the time they get there. This is

79

surely a strong objection to increasing the length of academic courses. By the time the student has reached the end, he will have absorbed the thought-processes of his predecessors so completely that he may react as violently as they would do to the revolutionary innovation which his science or technology is really demanding.

The problem is more easily formulated than the solution. Perhaps the development of the sandwich principle and a great increase in the number of 'delayed' post-graduate courses will encourage constructive activities to be undertaken earlier and so stave off the ossification of young minds, with its elimination of rebellious heterodoxy. Perhaps a wide diversification of first-degree courses will lead to a variety of end-products whose interplay will produce greater developments in research. A general degree has tended to be thought of as the retreat into which those not fitted to be front-line troops would slip; perhaps it will have to be re-assessed as the best training for staff officers, who must otherwise be ignorant about what half their men are doing. Philosophy has often been regarded as too vague and remote to be relevant preparation for a scientific career; perhaps—with some shift of emphasis—it will prove the most desirable background for a man thinking his way into a radically new situation. So the monopoly of the special science degree, with its attempt to sharpen intelligence solely by concentrating study in a narrow field, may be broken.

Ph.D.s

With a slight perversity, it seems to have been arranged that classification by titles occurs at just the wrong levels. Thus most people would agree that the sharper distinction comes between the honours degree and the pass degree, rather than between those who have and those who have not scraped a pass degree; yet all but the last can proudly call themselves Bachelors. Similarly, there is a wider gulf between the D.Sc. and the Ph.D. than between the latter and the man on the next lower rung, but at first glance the first two are both indistinguishably doctors.

The cynics might argue that the sole purpose of the Ph.D. degree is to correct some of the errors of the undergraduate courses that precede it. While the tradition, that the brightest of each year's graduates linger on to do research, means that the recruiting sergeant cannot ignore the Ph.D.s, it must be admitted that the young men in question are often less immediate use to an industrial laboratory at the end of those three years than they would have been had they spent them learning the ropes of industrial research. No doubt in the long run the wider horizons, given by university life at a slightly senior level, will bring their benefits. The present author's qualifications (and his admission, under pressure, of having gained a first-class honours degree in experimental physics before he had ever soldered two wires together) justify his repeating the story about the go-ahead firm that engaged a brilliant young scientist. Anxious to ensure his exclusive services for some years, they laid before him a comprehensive contract with a space for his signature, which he filled XX. Asked why, he explained that, since he could not write, he always put an X for his name—and the second X represented his Ph.D.

Memory

A vital question, which starts to be answered at school or even before, and is continuously extended through life, is what the memory shall be stored with. It is the biggest—though not the only—issue behind each battle over an examination syllabus. We would urge that the facts a scientist remembers should spread wide rather than contain detail. He must carry in his head the basic laws of his science, and it will help him to know rough values for the constants which keep recurring in his calculations. If his work involves mathematical manipulations, he will need to have memorised the techniques, for it would take too long to learn them again afresh for each operation. But it is really wasteful to be able to quote from memory either detailed formulae or precise numerical values. If he is to use these, it should be carefully and deliberately; trustworthy conclusions demand that the reasoning should be set out calmly and at leisure, which will provide adequate opportunity for checking quotations. Much more important is to remember the framework in which the matter is set, and the right place to look to find the answer written down. If you have remembered that some factor is relevant to your experiment, but don't know how, there are ways of finding out, but if you have forgotten that it comes in at all, your whole experiment may be invalidated without your knowing it. Again, when the memory is buttressed by a card index—as I believe all scientists' memories should be—it is scarcely necessary to remember a single thing that is on the cards; but woe betide the man who forgets the principles of classification he has used in deciding what goes where!

A special plea we would make—by no means applicable only to research workers—is for training in remembering people. It is an asset to almost anyone if faces and names can be readily recalled, and, while it may come naturally to some lucky ones, it seems likely that most folk could be disciplined into a habit of mind that is at least considerably better than the forgetfulness they will often have to admit to.

Intelligence and memorising

The similarity between a computer and the human brain is often pointed out. The parallelism is not always emphasised of the distinction in both cases between storage and operational facilities. The users of electronic computers have had a phase when they have had cause to bewail the lack of sufficient storage capacity. The human brain does not appear to be lacking in quite the same way: there is little evidence that, in the long run, the storage of some information will prevent the storage of other. Rather is the limitation set by the write-in time. This, of course, is where hard work comes in; by increasing the writing time—and perhaps the intensity of writing—more and more information can be recorded. The need for the hard work is aggravated, because it seems to be particularly burdensome to memorise things that we are not interested in—and it is difficult to maintain interest in an abstract mathematical result whose derivation was beyond our comprehension. One need certainly is to see that our work continues to prove interesting to us.

We may also note the interchangeability between memory-arising-from-hard-work and intelligence, particularly with regard to passing exams. The intelligent individual will get away with a minimum of memorised material, which he will process as necessary to produce the answers. The end-product is often indistinguishable from that served up by the less intelligent harder worker who has memorised the answers ready-made. On the whole, we are less interested in the extent of a man's memory, and it is to be hoped that examiners will learn to contrive questions that probe the operational rather than the storage side of the computer. There is a tendency that examinations of higher standards are, in fact, more searching of intelligence: dare we suggest that the Higher National Certificate represents the highest rung that can be reached simply on the strength of an uncomprehending memory?

While, therefore, the memory has its uses in a research lab. (and few things are more galling than the junior member of the team who insists on working things out wrongly for himself instead of remembering what he was told), the big advances and the success of the seniors depend more on other functions of the brain. Most important is that indefinable, easily recognisable thing called intelligence. It is dangerous for a layman to try to describe intelligence; he will be tempted to equate it with the characteristics that distinguish his friends—and himself—from his enemies! No doubt, intelligence tests are framed to escape from the unequal biassing of previous experience by confronting their subject with novel situations. This is just what the practice of a scientific career will do to him; and we would suggest that the ability to juggle mentally with the many factors that enter an experiment—or a sum—or a situation—until a solution is discerned is almost exactly the same thing as intelligence.

This raises the issue of speed of working (shades of an electronic computer, again). It is a great asset to be able to finish your thinking quickly; intruders into hostile committees, in particular, find it invaluable to realise the implications of various statements one jump ahead of their neighbours, so as to bend the direction of the subsequent conversation accordingly. In parenthesis, beware of underestimating the lag with which they may be following you, or half your remarks may seem irrelevant because the implications that were obvious to you were undetectable by them. But more fundamental is the question whether rate of thinking and ultimate profundity of thinking are distinguishable or whether they are simply different aspects of the same thing. It might be thought that genius is merely the ability to review many possibilities in rapid succession, to apply each of the pieces from the box to the mental jigsaw puzzle being studied, in which case it would belong strictly with quick thinking. We would be inclined to distinguish, and to claim that some individuals go more deeply into a problem than their colleagues who might, however, get such answers as they are capable of much more quickly. Computers have circuit subtleties as well as clock rates.

Temperament

Thus far, we have dealt with matters of the intellect rather than the emotions. In this materialistic age, there is a feeling about that it is only the giant brains that matter; no longer will sweet maids be recommended to be good and leave the cleverness to those who will: if you are bright enough, you may be a boor. Unfortunately, this last is, humanly speaking, true; but the threshold luminosity is very high. Those who do not reach such pinnacles of unique contributions to science that they cannot be ignored will have to work with others and submit to their criticism and discipline; therefore their temperament is important. What contributes to it?

One item that cannot be ignored is just this reaction to criticism. The essence of scientific method is that every idea should appear before the bar of experiment: experimental confirmation or refutation is the only ultimate authority, and is certainly a higher court than human opinion. This is in contrast with a great many human activities, where the uniqueness of the situation prevents an experiment being carried out so that a reliance on opinions cannot be avoided. In politics or in business, for instance, the precise world situation will never be repeated, so it cannot be conclusively demonstrated what another course of action would have led to. Even in engineering, if it is on a large scale, it is not generally practicable to duplicate approaches. It follows that decisions must be based on human judgment, and the humans who make those judgments achieve a consequential authority. In the scientific world, by contrast, the arbiter of experiment deals (more or less) impartially with fresh raw student and with F.R.S. The right to criticise has therefore come to be recognised, and the right to invalidate cherished theories by impertinent experiments has spilled over into the right to point out flaws in logic, and even, partially and illogically, into the temerity to comment on programmes of work. But beware, junior readers, lest you act too confidently and too tactlessly on the assumption that your bosses will accept all this when it comes to the acid test of practice!

It will, therefore, make a great difference to a man's value in research if he can step outside himself and listen dispassionately to his colleagues. This holds when they are discussing the soundness of his ideas. It also holds when the priority of his ideas is in dispute. For a research worker is either lucky or dull if he gets far through his career without some clash of opinions as to who was responsible for initiating something. Very few ideas grow to their full stature in a single mind. The great majority gain most value by shuttling from one individual to another, and even at their conception, parthenogenesis is probably rarer than cross-fertilisation. At the same time, a natural egotism always emphasises in our own minds the contribution that we ourselves have made. It is not surprising, therefore, that there

85

should often be divergences of view. To be able to listen calmly and sympathetically to the other man's claims is a great asset. A greater is the ability to take it philosophically when he has stolen a march on you with a claim which you know passes unjustifiably over those things that you have been responsible for*. Occasionally you will even find that you should be glad at his assuming the authorship of an idea, because then and only then will it receive his necessary support!

While we would repeatedly stress the importance of temperament to a scientist's overall value, this is certainly not to say that there is a single, absolute specification to which he must conform. It may often be that either extreme of character is preferable to a lukewarm mediocrity—though an artificial extremity of character is probably worst of all. There is undoubtedly room in the laboratory for the patient, painstaking individual who will continue to accumulate results with commendable thoroughness and aggravating slowness, as well as for the restless personality continually seeking new worlds to invade and reluctant to spend time on mopping up operations. Enthusiasm, whether exuberant or profound, and humility, whether in high intellectual flights or lowly, are the cardinal, indispensable virtues. Covet them earnestly, if you would contribute to science rather than merely advance your own career.

Malevolent nature

One aspect of humility concerns estimating the probable success of a line of action that has been conceived. This may be a vast, many-sided project or a trivial laboratory detail, but in any such estimating it is imperative to assume that Nature is ag'in' you— that if there is any loophole of uncertainty you have left in your planning, it will turn out unfavourably! While this may sound

---

* J. D. Bernal, *The Social Function of Science*, Routledge, London, 1939, p. 84. Lindor Brown, *The Perils of Leadership in Science*, Oxford University Press, London, 1960, p. 11.

86

like a heathen philosophy of the malevolence of Nature, it is of course really a way of discounting an inherent sub-conscious optimism. By personalising (and slandering) the opposition we transfer and project the errors of our own conceit. Akin to this is the approach that must be adopted when our apparatus seems to present us with a contradiction; on the face of it, our results indicate that we have disproved some fundamental and cherished Law—generations of gullible scientists have evidently been kidding themselves. Then it is necessary to creep up on Nature in very small steps, establishing for certain each of the points that we have expected and assumed to be true. At the end, we will either have established a basic new principle, or—in 99 cases out of 100!—have realised that we were misled somewhere along the line. This, I believe, holds for large matters and for small, for theorising and for experiment, for engineering rules of thumb as well as for fundamental laws.

Advantages of newcomers

An element of scepticism, an engrained refusal to accept that you are right until you are logically compelled to do so, is thus a valuable weapon in the armoury of research. But the rarity of striking success should not blind us to its possibility. That, after all, is what we are primarily there for, and the value of marginal improvements and refinements must not mask the much greater potential wealth of the revolutionary concept and the radical innovation. The sub-conscious disbelief in drastic changes, which the old hand so often has, is largely why such a good record is held by newcomers to a subject. The history, ancient and modern, of Science gives many instances of far-reaching discoveries made by research workers originally trained in a different discipline, and a study of important inventions brings it out even more clearly*. Of course, there are several factors contributing to this. The most enterprising people in any field will include those most

---

* J. Jewkes et al., The Sources of Invention, Macmillan, London, 1958.

"Specialists arriving from either side of the frontier may well cross into each other's territory"

likely to have the initiative to change. The most rapidly developing parts of science are commonly those where, according to the old classification, two subjects meet; and the specialists arriving from either side of the frontier may well cross into each other's territory. Therefore, even the ambitious young scientist would be ill-advised to change his field of study drastically every year or two, in the hope of finding a personal Eldorado. Rather should he apply the lesson of our repeated—and obvious—counsel that he should think widely, without preconceptions, and then judge dispassionately.

Creativity

We have already referred in passing to the quality that is called creativity. There may be uncertainty whether it should be ranked as an aspect of cold intellect or whether thought of as a matter of emotion and temperament, but there can be no questioning that it is of supreme importance in research, and justifies further attention. Creation should be defined as bringing into existence or forming out of nothing ('creation' of matter from radiation is thus a misnomer, although—for the present—the cosmologists' continuous 'creation' is rightly so called). It is only in the abstract that humankind can have any facility for creation. It may be arguable, even there, how far the newly arising idea has a parentage of earlier ideas. But undoubtedly there are some original thoughts that do not seem to follow, as natural sequels, on what has gone before: a jump has taken place. If we draw the parallel between a computer and human thinking, this is where it breaks down; for a computer can only act—albeit at unprecedented speeds—in a predictable way according to what has been fed into it. And on occasions, at least to all appearances, the human mind does more. When it has been told to select the best of several alternatives, it sometimes goes outside its terms of reference and points out that something not on the list is best of all. It introduces radical innovation.

This, of course, is the very essence of scientific research. By the perception of new and wider relations, by the realisation that supposedly axiomatic objections are invalid, science advances. Nor is it only in the highest flights that creativity is important. The results, of course, are more striking when fundamental concepts are overturned, but every working scientist needs something of the spark of originality if his labours are not to degenerate into routine hackwork. A laboratory will soon go flat and flavourless if it lacks this essential leaven, and the first requirement from its recruiting activities is that they should provide for a continuous succession of creativity. In conceiving nuclear models or the mechanism of heredity, we need creativity; but also in devising pipettes or computer circuits, in planning new ways of measuring old variables or in contriving one experiment to give the results of two. Perhaps it is the same basic quality that suggests new fields of enterprise to the businessman or new avenues of approach to the diplomat; if, so, then a scramble between the professions for their common requirement of raw material is inevitable, and, as we have said, the casual selection of subjects—and hence of destinations—at school becomes of great significance.

We may ask whether creativity is born or instilled in a man. The answer is probably that both are necessary. There are many individuals who give the impression that however they had been reared, no matter what rare inspiring influences had played upon them, they could never have given birth to a markedly original idea. But there is also a danger that even those possessed of an incipient creativity may have it stifled by the compulsion of impressed orthodoxy for too long. It may not be possible to create creativity, but it is sadly possible to annihilate it.

While we stress how indispensable sources of new ideas are for live research work, it must not be thought that they are all that matter. It will be very seldom that all the new ideas are good, and a filtration process must be applied to eliminate the unprofitable. If much of the filtering can be done by the originator, much less ill-feeling will be caused than if it must all be by an external judge. So that the ability to assess the absurdity of a new proposal, even one's own, is a most valuable concomitant to the ability to generate one. Often, a multi-stage filter is advantageous, so that the completely absurd is disposed of quickly while those that are only just impracticable are debated for longer. In fact, on many occasions it will be found useful to have the habit of quickly classifying ideas into three categories: obviously good, obviously bad and requiring further thought. Of course, the greater the output of ideas, the greater the strain on the filters, so that—to make free with the metaphors—while mental fertilisation is often a popular catchword, it must be admitted that some minds are in greater need of weed-killer than of fertiliser.

Emotional involvement

Presumably, all professional people have to face the issue of how far they should become personally involved emotionally in the matters they handle from day to day. The lawyer, at one extreme, must remain completely detached. The artist, at the other extreme, has surely to involve his own personality if his artistry is not to ring hollow. The doctor, the soldier, perhaps especially the clergyman come agonisingly between, having at times to suffer a sharp tension between the call for them to be embroiled with sympathy in the sufferings of those they serve and the need to stand a little outside in contact with stable authority. At first thought, we might assign the scientist a position alongside the lawyer, assessing matters with a cold intellect and banishing all emotion as irrelevant. But this would be to shut our eyes to the manner of human working. It just is not possible for an idea to be followed up with the drive necessary to establish it unless there is an element of emotional involvement in the matter. Without an intense wish that the newly propounded theory will be justified, or the new technique prove practicable, a sense of motive will be missing from a laboratory and the work there will languish into torpor. This is true for the effort of one man; it is doubly true for the labours of a team.

We have, however, the dilemma that the intense personal concern in a project, the need to support it with something of the

$$\text{``}\frac{\mathrm{d}F}{\mathrm{d}t} = \left(\frac{\mathrm{d}F}{\mathrm{d}t}\right)_{\!\circ} + k\left[\frac{\mathrm{d}\pounds}{\mathrm{d}t} - \left(\frac{\mathrm{d}\pounds}{\mathrm{d}t}\right)_{\!\circ}\right]\text{''}$$

enthusiasm lavished on boat races and cup ties, must not warp judgment of its soundness, This, surely, is the major problem facing the research worker as he formulates his approach to his job: he must give his emotions sufficient rein to provide him with strong motivation for wrestling with the difficulties facing him, while remembering that they must never have the final say in decisions of any magnitude. Perhaps this is just a slight shift from that description of the British attitude to life which says that it demands that everything be treated as a joke, the greatest joke of all being that the joker is really in dead earnest. Perhaps the blend of emotion and intellect indicates that the creative scientist is not really so far removed from the creative artist.

Health

We might wonder whether the tension between emotional motivation and intellectual restraint would lead to psychological disorders. They are not unknown in laboratories, but neither have they been shown to be more frequent there than elsewhere. The scientist's health problems are no different from those of other responsible thinkers: the occupational diseases that might have developed in him have been carefully anticipated and eliminated by disinterested scientists! All that is left is for him to study the orthodox advice to managerial types. He might laugh hollowly and point out that exercise, E and eating, dF/dt are related to salary, $d\pounds/dt$ by

$$E \propto 1 \left/ \frac{d\pounds}{dt} \right. \text{ and } \frac{dF}{dt} = \left(\frac{dF}{dt}\right)_{o} + k\left[\frac{d\pounds}{dt} - \left(\frac{d\pounds}{dt}\right)_{o}\right]$$

while at least some managerial sickness, S_m, is a function

$$S_m \propto \frac{dF/dt}{E} - \left(\frac{dF/dt}{E}\right)_{\text{crit.}}$$

At least, the scientist, being a rational individual, will have weighed up the situation and realised the great importance of health. His body, with all its faculties, physical and mental, must

93

be brought into subjection and shaped to the ideal; but whether he could dare to be explicit in describing that ideal is another matter. The norm, any departure from which is equivalent to illness, is indefinable.

The citation index production gauge

All such factors of health and temperament concern us because of their bearing on the 'research output' of a man. A difficulty is that in this field of human activity productivity is exceptionally difficult to gauge. I was told that, in pre-war Russia, research laboratory employees were paid piece-work rates like everybody else, but I have never discovered how this was done. The subjective impression one gains is that, in research, productivity can vary between one man and another by a wider ratio than in almost any other field. But if we try (following the good Kelvinian approach) to measure this elusive quality, we find it impossible just because of the continually changing situation in which research is carried out. Who can say, in any one situation, whether a research worker found no answer to his problem because he was dull or because at that time it was insoluble? Is the man credited with the big discovery really a genius or only the lucky individual who happens to put the crowning touch on an edifice of cumulative ideas? But even apart from that, how do we say which is the big discovery? It seems to be tragically easy for individuals, and even whole laboratories, to carry on for years with an output that has very little value to anyone.

In some circles this is counteracted by an insistence on publication. The onus for deciding whether what has been submitted is worth publishing is passed to the editors and referees of the technical journals. Of course, there is some safeguard here. If he has produced a conclusion definite enough to write a paper around it, the working scientist cannot have idled his time away completely. He has produced some answer to some question. Whether that question was worth answering may be more difficult to decide. Under most laboratory structures, the responsibility for the question rests at a higher level than the responsibility for the answer—and the higher level may be less willing to be probed searchingly! Moreover, it is being increasingly realised that a blind emphasis on quantity of output in the shape of papers leads to a proliferation of writing that is already in danger of choking the channels of scientific communication.

The assessment of productivity that is needed, as a first improvement on one man's judgment, is something like the considered verdict of the whole scientific community. This cannot be given quickly—in the very nature of things, a delayed verdict will be better because it takes account of subsequent developments; it is generally accepted in instrumentation circles that if you cannot have a quick-response meter, one with a slow response will still be a great deal better than nothing.

I would suggest that we have a way of assessing the mature opinion of the scientific community—an output meter ready to hand—if we count up, not a man's own publications but the number of times they are referred to in other people's publications. Let us have a *Citation Index Production Gauge*, which uses the number of times a man's papers are quoted to indicate the value of the research he has done.

Such a count of references could, in fact, become a powerful analytical tool. It would be capable of refinement. A reference in a more learned journal could score more, while particular weight could be given to crossing international boundaries. There is a slight risk of collusion: two parties might have a mutual understanding that they would each repeatedly refer to the work of the other. But there is a broadly accepted standard of when and when not to give a reference to somebody else's research. Compared with the deliberate incitement to the production of unworthy articles, that is implicit in the current, fortunately restricted, practice of judging quality by quantity of publication, the new proposal is impeccable.

At first sight, the labour involved in collecting references might seem prohibitive. However, as people got into the habit of listing references appropriately, the task could well become acceptable. When librarians are superseded by computers, there would be little objection to insisting that they prepared one extra set of indices. We may note the vast effort that goes into financial accounting; for a research laboratory, several men may do nothing all day except make entries that allow the books to be balanced. With meticulous care it is recorded exactly which pocket the incoming monies were placed in, and from which pocket payment was made. But the end-product of it all, the real purpose for which the cash travelled in and round and out, is left completely un-valued—not only in absolute terms, but even in the relative manner that would enable one output to be compared with another.

There are dangers in applying the idea too widely. Probably more cross-referencing is to be expected in purer scientific work than in technology. In the former, a close-knit fabric of know-ledge is being built up, while in the latter some brilliant, pioneer-ing technique may be copied a hundred times with no published acknowledgments. Some laboratories are bound by secrecy—but few people would object to any procedure that contained an encouragement to them to minimise that secrecy.

As between comparable individuals and comparable establish-ments, valid conclusions could undoubtedly be drawn. There would be a large measure of random variations, but if, as I suspect, research productivities often differ by orders of magni-tude, then this would be expected to show up in the citation index. A repeated low score by a laboratory would be the signal for its sponsors to raise their eye-brows. With an individual, counting the references to his work should, for the first time, enable a fair picture to be obtained of the variation of his pro-ductivity through his life-cycle. As a by-product different journals could be compared: some mischievous character could even check whether *Proc. Roy. Soc.* justified its vaunted pre-eminence.

We have mentioned the time lag in getting a citation index assessment. This could itself be studied. In Fig. 12, we show several (hypothetical) curves relating the number of references to a paper to the time when they were made. The total area under

96

the curve is, of course, *A*, the simple citation index figure of merit. Curve 1 refers to a discovery that just met needs that had been building up round the world; perhaps it was a new experimental technique that broke through previous limitations or perhaps it was a theory that accounted for a back-log of unexplained experimental results. Curve 2 is for a book that surveyed the field so soundly that for years no successor was required. The

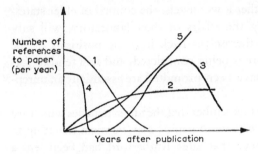

Fig. 12. References to a paper at different time lags after publication.

subject of curve 3 was a bit ahead of its time: it was some years before the rest of the world caught up with the importance of the work. The explanation of curve 4 is that the startling results were shown to be phoney when other people repeated them, while curve 5, like all divergent ones, is a clear sign of genius.

Scientists beware. The back pages of *Nature* may soon include phrases such as: "Applications (ten copies) should include a list of the applicant's publications together with a further list of other publications where they are quoted—and if possible a third list of publications quoting the quoters".

Apeing the great

The case for citation index production gauges, and indeed for many other matters, is likely to be argued with the behaviour of famous scientists in mind. There may well be the tacit assumption that because Lord So-and-so acted in such-and-such a way, or

97

because some particular procedure would have helped the recorded inventor of an important new process, we can draw valid conclusions for the treatment of Tom, Dick and Harry at the lab. bench. But can we? Is it valid, as well as attractive, to buttress an argument with illustrations from history? Sir Ambrose Fleming, as a consultant, said that his F.R.S. stood for Fees Raised Since, and again that Knightwork was paid double rate—but were these the only respects in which he was different from lesser mortals? Even at rather lower levels, the council of elder statesmen, when debating the affairs of their laboratory, will subconsciously project themselves back into the positions of the juniors whose welfare is being considered, and will tend to forget that they who have been promoted are essentially an unrepresentative sample.

Those juniors must remember that the idiosyncracies which are tolerable, or even welcome in genius may be most irritating in other people. I believe that after Rutherford had been lent a strong radioactive source by the Vienna Academy of Science, they tried vainly at least once to get it returned. We may smile at his brushing aside their request, but only because we know that he is going to employ the radium to revolutionise atomic physics: woe betide you if you hold on to my oscilloscope—which you are using rather wastefully anyhow!

On the other hand, we cannot deny that there is much in common between true scientists of all levels of ability, so that the extreme cases will often merely point more sharply the morals that are also applicable elsewhere. Moreover, each laboratory must remember that the real stray genius crossing its threshold may make a greater contribution to science than all the rest of its staff put together. Just as the administration of justice should be devised to protect the innocent even at the risk of the guilty sometimes escaping, so the administration of research must allow genius to flourish even if ordinary folk occasionally run riot as a consequence.

98

Writing with the acclamations for the first cosmonautrix still almost ringing in the ears, it is difficult to suggest that there can be much necessary difference between the mental calibre of the sexes. Perhaps the Russians really have demonstrated that parity is possible, with the corollary that Britain's girls' schools constitute her largest untapped reservoir for increased scientific personnel.

But it must not be concluded that the situation can be changed overnight—nor even that we necessarily want such a solution; for it must never be assumed that the total purpose of human organisation on earth is to increase scientific research effort. The situation at present facing scientists, scientistes and employers in this country is very different from that in Russia, even if the difference is not so much congenital as the result of training. Indeed, we have already shown how our educational system can bring about the perpetuation of an attitude. It does seem broadly true that women have less facility than men in the more rigorous logical processes associated with the so-called exact sciences. This may be compensated for in the realm of descriptive science, or perhaps the balance is only redressed when we reach the humanities and arts. Of greater importance in the practical running of any research establishment is the undoubted feminine skill at delicate manipulations. This may well stem partly from the broader principle that to a woman, business activities—with all the ambitions and schemings and jealousies they are apt to involve— are of less importance than to a man. For a given intellectual capacity, therefore, she will be content to do more mundane work, be it routine titrations, laborious computations or threading invisibly fine wire through incredibly small holes. The obverse of this coin is a disinclination to accept responsibility. It is only in the affairs that most deeply concern us that we are willing to undertake the real burden of real responsibility—as distinct from the quick assumption of authority that may come automatically to some natures. When, therefore, a woman, consciously or sub-

99

consciously, rates homes and people in them as more important than workplaces and their contents, she will not be able to be sufficiently absorbed in a laboratory to justify high promotion there. Many would go on to say that this corresponds to a fundamental biological distinction, that it is more natural for women to accept a role of obedience to men than *vice versa*.

But always remember the large fluctuations within a sample of the population of either sex, which will often make nonsense of applying generalisations to particular cases. Moreover, with the tradition and climate in this country set markedly against the entry of girls into certain technical fields, it will be found that those who have had the nerve to break through into the forbidden territory must be possessed of determination and an enthusiasm for their subject.

To drive home these and other points, we quote two poems*. They were provoked by a quotation urging teachers to encourage girls to take up science, and deal with the motivation behind the probable brevity of a young woman's appointment, the aspect of the subject that has often dominated discussion elsewhere to the exclusion of other considerations.

> Though science and industry open their arms
>   To welcome the female trainee,
> Girls feel they would waste those endearing young charms
>   By taking a science degree.
>
> The girl of today is not seizing her chance,
>   Let her teachers appeal as they will—
> She feels that the lab. is no road to romance,
>   So she'll stay a stenographer still.
>
> Though offered a new scientific career,
>   Should she pore over sums night and day,
> And as chemist, technician, or trained engineer,
>   See her loveliness fading away?

* I am grateful to *Mercutio* and *The Guardian* for permission to reproduce the first. To my regret, I have not been able to trace the author of the second.

Why should she her brain-power increase, just to share
　　Some underpaid scientist's life,
When by taking down letters with average care
　　She might end as the manager's wife?

Advance in technology now must be made,
　　And woman can play her full part;
But a knowledge of physics and maths is no aid
　　To winning the masculine heart.

For sticking to shorthand she may be to blame;
　　Her choice is a national loss,
But she will not be turned from her personal aim,
　　Which is simply—to marry the boss.

— — — — — — —

As science and industry open their arms
　　To welcome the female trainee,
Then so do the scientists, snared by the charms
　　Of the girl with the science degree.

For who would be one of a typewriting pool
　　With a heart pumping fast as the keys,
When the manager halts at a neighbouring stool,
　　Which is draped with more glamorous knees?

In a lab. there's one girl to each dozen of men:
　　While the scarcity lasts here's her chance.
The test-tube is mightier far than the pen,
　　For attracting the amorous glance.

A scientist's salary may not be grand
　　But he'll yield to the gentlest push,
And to capture a four-figure boff-in the hand
　　Is worth five figures still in the bush.

The modern girl calculates well and she'll vote
　　For a safe scientific career:
Matrimonial prospects are far from remote
　　And a patriot she will appear.

So she'll look at her teachers with innocent eyes
　　And agree to the course they suggest,
Protesting her loyalty, sure of her prize—
　　For boffins like boffinettes best!

— — — — — — —

These then, are some reflections on the characteristics of research workers, and the causes and consequences of those characteristics. 'Know thyself' has been wise advice for many years: then you will be able to effect desirable changes, or at least to allow in your calculations for what cannot or will not be changed.

We would extend the advice to include knowledge of one's fellows. This, in fact, is a surprisingly important element in the settling-in period in any new job. It is desirable to know which typist has had a rudimentary scientific education, and which storekeeper insists, whenever he is in doubt, that he has no stocks of the goods he is asked for. The compilation of a list of ten-minute consultants can extend over a life-time: the subjects of consultations may range from Laplace transforms to the best route into the middle of Birmingham. One column in the consultancy table will touch on the conciseness of the answer given, so that, for those with low marks here, care can be taken to approach them only a few minutes before they have another pressing engagement.

We must learn which of our colleagues are prepared to put themselves out to help us; we must learn which have influence in high places. Above all, we must learn the reliability of their answers. There are some who tolerance their own replies, and tell us the weight to attach to them, but for some we must always add *sotto voce*, that this is what they think at the moment, with correction factors to be added according to the wish-paternity of the thought and according to the rosiness of today's spectacles.

5. How?

The art of research

It may well be thought that the question *How* to do research should bring the most substantial answers of any in this book. Where it is carried out, and who do the carrying (let alone whither) are perhaps secondary problems that may be left to solve themselves. But many would agree that the justification for *The Art of Research* comes if, and only if it can throw some light on the way in which research should be done. It is a truism nowadays that the volume of research work grows apace. The wheels of the machine of higher education are being slowly but continuously accelerated to train the coming generations of researchers. But their textbooks are almost exclusively taken up with descriptions of Nature and codes of practice for engineering. True, they contain accounts of new techniques—though these sometimes seem slower to find their way to print than the results they have produced, perhaps from their originators' understandable wish to maintain a lead. Thus the budding scientist is furnished with some knowledge of the material tools available, but he is given little guidance about the mental, or human approach. We should think it odd if the subject of *Education* were eliminated from the curricula of our Teaching Training Colleges, under the argument that it was only necessary to absorb the subject being taught, and an appreciation of the techniques of teaching would follow automatically. It seems equally strange that, for the most part, we concentrate on making our researchers acquainted with the present state of knowledge, which is to form their jumping off point. We take it for granted that some instinct will guide them how to set about extending this knowledge—although the dozen generations since modern science made its debut can scarcely have been sufficient for natural selection to have bred such a novelty!

One of the reasons for neglecting such teaching has no doubt been its difficulty. We have suggested before that research is an art, and the essence of art is not easy to trap in the confines of a textbook. The professional scientist, particularly, whose business is to couch his ideas in precise phrases, may find it against his training to have to express the inexact concepts of how to do research.

This may mean that personal examples are the best lessons. But there are not many of the top rank available, and most of them are working on a different scale from our raw beginner— and we cannot, anyhow, be quite sure that the approach adopted by the genius should be that for the more lowly. A Master Surgeon may still stride through hospital wards at the head of a posse of students; but, if research is to be learned that way, the queue winding through the senior offices of our laboratories, watching to see the great men think, would completely obstruct effective administration.

So, a chapter of thoughts about the matters that arise when deciding how to do research, may be very soundly justified.

Literature surveys

About the first thing, when given a research problem to do, is to see what other people have already done about it. This is not simply to make sure that nobody has got in ahead of you, solving your particular problem. There are sure to be many gaps in your knowledge of related subjects that will need to be plugged before you can soundly launch out on a programme of your own devising.

The routine procedure is to start with text books and work down to increasingly specialised fields. At the broadest phase, library catalogues and classifications will give a lead what to read. Some libraries offer a more detailed service. Many can quote a large number of references without being able to say how relevant or how comprehensive they are, but such offerings are certainly not to be despised. For, in general, there is no such thing as absolute comprehensiveness, although our finite minds have a longing for it, and the belief keeps on asserting itself that there must be some document, or some person, that contains all the answers. The sounder approach is to recognise incompleteness elsewhere, and to adopt the resolute aim that the scientist himself, applying his diligence to his chosen field, shall become the comprehensive reference list. The justification for so thinking himself will come, or be gradually approached, only by following up the variety of leads that are presented to him.

The better, bigger books will contain references to other, more detailed sources, which can be traced. The parallel procedure is to use abstract journals—or files of abstract cards—and follow them back through the years, looking up the appropriate subjects in their indices. It is most important to be systematic. I believe that there is no effective substitute for a private card index; if this can err on the side of being over-elaborate, it will encourage the compiler to take a personal pride in it, almost for its own sake, and this will offset the tendency towards skimping that human lethargy is tempted to. Thought should be given to the classification system. If this is primarily by subject (but probably with no more than a distant family likeness to the Universal Decimal Classification), it will automatically be unique to its owner, reflecting the individuality of his interests—and perhaps hinting at the history of his development. The order within a class may be by author's name, which is often a simple means of identification when other things are only half-remembered. The date of the publication is also of primary importance. A colour code, or something similar, could allow this to be quickly recognised.

Delays in laying hands on obscure journals, and inability to solve the puzzles posed by incorrectly quoted references, will prevent the reading target from ever being reached, for widening interests should add to the list at a rate that must eventually give equilibrium with the papers that are being read plus those abandoned as not quite essential reading after all. If too high a standard is persevered in, and nothing abandoned, the would-be researcher will find that he has degenerated into a reading machine.

Thus, literature surveys are continuous, interminable operations. They are not the only way of becoming acquainted with other people's achievements, and they should be parallelled by discussions with experts. Such discussions can give a feel for the latest way of thinking in pure science or an acquaintance with the latest techniques in the technologies. In fact, an established scientist can generally bring the novice along to a point of knowledgability in much less time than he would take by wading through the literature. But it is not fair to expect the expert to give up his time repeating the fundamentals that could be acquired from print. A basic background must be built up the hard way, to which a superstructure can then be added by discussion with the expert. Only those of considerable eminence can reasonably ask to have a personally conducted expedition from the lowlands of their own elementary education right out to the pinnacles of knowledge. So the process will go on, of reading, hearing, thinking, assimilating; so the research worker must keep himself informed of world progress, both before and while he makes his own contribution to it.

Analysis of problems

As the literature survey goes on, the phase of problem analysis also builds up. At first, the enquirer necessarily examines other people's work with an absolutely open mind, not only as to the results of their experiments and calculations, but even concerning the framework in which these are set—whether the right questions, from his point of view, are being tackled. A little later, as the research worker grapples with his own task, he will come back to the literature with more specific questions in his mind that need answering.

The process of analysing the problem and how to tackle it is undoubtedly of great importance. It is where the good scientist demonstrates his worth. For sound work here ensures that subsequent time is well spent, while faulty or uninspired thinking at this stage can result in months of work that eventually prove quite unproductive. There is, therefore, justification for having the most talented people that are available, and several of them, to give their minds to the subject, provided—and it is a severe proviso—that 'talented' in this context is taken to include an adequate familiarity with all the details of the subject.

The process of analysing the situation will vary widely from case to case. It may include some estimate of whether it is really worth doing anything about it at all, the relative priority to be given to theoretical and experimental approaches and whether adequate tools are already available or whether a major proportion of the initial effort will be indirect, devoted to developing techniques. If several different factors are liable to influence the phenomenon studied, ways of disentangling their effects will be considered. For many problems, a tentative hypothesis to explain what is observed should be sought as soon as possible: this will give direction and motivation for proposing particular studies, and if there is a readiness to abandon untenable positions, no harm is done by starting with something that is highly speculative. A great deal of applied research is aimed at showing how phenomena that are observed in certain situations follow naturally from accepted basic laws. If the phenomena are at first sight surprising, then there must be some unexpected way in which the basic laws take effect. Part of the skill of analysis lies in selecting the right law for following through in detail.

Much research that is called fundamental follows the same procedure. The very fundamental scientist, however, will occasionally have the joy of introducing a completely new concept, and showing that when he applies this, in a way that can command a measure of respect from his fellows, he can predict the previously unpredictable.

Sometimes, of course, the problem presented is smaller and

more trivial than would seem to justify any analysis on the scale we have indicated. Sometimes it will be an extension of an earlier investigation, for which the background thinking will already have been done. We would urge, however, that some phase of analysis should always be passed through, in order to avoid journeys up cul-de-sacs, even up short ones.

Thunderstruck drosophila—an example

Let us outline how our reading and analysis for a typical problem might go. Consider the hypothetical study, already mentioned, of the effects of lightning upon *drosophila*. We have shown how the scientist's approach can be modified by his personal inclinations, but if he is of sufficient calibre he will start by considering the whole wide sweep of possibilities. He will read about lightning, remembering that he must have a broad understanding of his whole subject. He will pay more attention to the quantitative description of lightning phenomena than to the theories of their origin. Similarly, his delving into the literature on *drosophila* will concentrate less on their ecology than on finding sensitive points in their physiology. He is likely to dismiss both the evolutionary background of *drosophila* and the geographical distribution of thunderstorms as irrelevant, though keeping in the back of his mind the possibility of a scoop in the shape of his own new Muggins Theory, which demonstrates how the one has influenced the other. His reading will have spread out into the nebulous area of how organisms generally are affected by electric—and possibly sound—fields, and here he will have to exercise considerable judgment as to how far he is justified in going.

As his book-learning builds up, he will be forming plans as to the original contribution he can most profitably make himself. This might be purely theoretical, taking published figures for the fundamentals on the one side—the electric fields that arise—and relating them to the fundamentals on the other side, such as the quantum-mechanical forces holding bio-molecules together. He might decide on a course of observation, noting particular aspects of the habits of *drosophila* in natural, or nearly natural situations. He might, again, embark on a series of experiments, subjecting the poor creatures (or possibly some related, more easily handled organism) to conditions that were highly artificial, but from which wider conclusions might be drawn. Very likely, the answer would be that all three lines should be followed simultaneously, for field work is likely to be long drawn out, with intervals (such as between the thunderstorms) that will be tedious and frustrating unless effort can be switched to a slightly different attack, while the development of original theory can give motivation and objectivity to reading, as well as filling in smaller intervals that would otherwise be idle. Note that, in the choice between various approaches, there is a delightful intermingling of judgments on different planes: an assessment of mathematical feasibility comes into it, as does the validity of extrapolation from one biological situation to another; human motivations of all the parties concerned must play a large part, and the avoidance of human foibles may forbid access to a technically promising field of study. The aim in all the planning will be to get the maximum results for the minimum work; simple experiments leading to limited conclusions may therefore be preferred to their opposites, but the man who persists too long in such an opportunist's path is in danger of being overtaken ultimately by the longer-winded. It is considerations like these that make the analysis of possible approaches to a scientific problem such a fascinating exercise.

In outlining the case of the thunderstruck *drosophila*, we have not touched on what we had said was the first consideration—whether the work was worth doing at all. Unfortunately, if any thought is given to this question, a firm negative will almost certainly render valueless all the subsequent cogitations that we have been through.

Inaccuracy

One matter that should feature prominently in the initial analysis of a scientific problem—and should recur again and again as the work develops—is the accuracy expected to be required. Far too little attention is normally paid to this, whereas the subconscious reaction to almost any proposal should be: 'How roughly can I do it and still get a worthwhile result?' Nernst is quoted by Mendelssohn* as having once said jokingly that no effect requiring more than 10% accuracy of measurement merited investigation.

Devise any of a wide range of experiments, and you will find that the time and the money you spend are doubled as you cut your errors down from ten percent to five. Pick up most instruments that are nominally good to two per cent, and they will very likely need a charitable interpretation even to reach that figure. Find the major source of error in the instrument and cure it, and you will probably discover that you have uncovered a host of slightly lesser errors: in fact, the maker has done a sound commercial job of work, wasting none of that precious commodity, cheapness, for things that he is not so sure will be acceptable. So covet earnestly acceptable inaccuracy. If cornered by your analysis, and compelled to admit that the third significant figure is important, see if you can escape from the extreme rigours of the demand by eliminating the need for absolute accuracy, depending only on the more reliable comparative figures.

Similarly, when theorising, it is exceptional for the last stage of precision and rigour to be desirable. Often because the mathematical techniques are complicated or absent; sometimes because it will be a laborious business to decide what values to use for the constants that must be inserted; almost always because it will take unnecessarily long. While the work leading to a rough calculation may be less, in quantity, it may, of course, demand higher quality. The assessment whether an approximation is legitimate may make greater demands on a man than the labourer, used to patiently foot-slogging his long division, can fulfil. Two or three years ago, a Common Entrance Examination paper included an item:

* K. MENDELSSOHN, The Meaning of Superfluidity, *New Scientist*, 23 (1964) 772–775.

"In this question *rough estimates* only are required and NO MARKS WILL BE GIVEN FOR WORKING IT ALL OUT..." but I believe it caused consternation among the Prep. School masters. Their boys could add, yes, but to recognise quickly the value of $267 + 58,977 — 123 + 11.72$ to the nearest 10,000—that demanded insight, and that was different. Long live the examiners.

Even if the development of the work may finally lead to an insistence on high accuracy, it generally pays to postpone the operation by embarking first on a pilot project that is a less close approximation. Such an undertaking will generally be so much easier that, even if it is later rendered superfluous by the more exact operation, the total effort expended will only be fractionally increased. On the other hand, it is quite possible that the pilot project will bring to light unforeseen aspects of the problem that make it quite valueless anyhow—or that make the lower accuracy perfectly acceptable.

No doubt this is partly a matter of temperament—and I am temperamentally an anti-accurist. There will always be scope for some who attend meticulously to detail, to extend precision or to uncover discrepancy. In contrast to Nernst, Michelson last century quoted "an eminent physicist" that "the future truths of Physical Science are to be looked for in the sixth place of decimals". Some will enjoy looking there, but I for one am glad that the search elsewhere is still far from exhausted.

Theory or experiment

We have considered the matter of accuracy first, because it arises with either approach, but it could well be argued that a more fundamental decision lies between the theoretical and the experimental attack on a problem—whether to measure or to calculate the answer. Sometimes it is obvious that one or the other is out of the question; sometimes it is clear that they must proceed equally and simultaneously. Quite often, however, there is at least a measure of choice where the emphasis should be laid. Faced with the question: What happens under such-and-such particular circumstances?—and questions like these make up a very large proportion of scientific research—we can choose whether we calculate it, working outward from known laws that we hope are relevant or whether we measure what is observed under conditions assumed to be similar.

The theoretician uses brain, exclusively of hand and eye. Perhaps that is the higher calling, though he can no longer scorn the experimenter for the latter's need to supplement body with lens or lever, since his own grey matter will very likely be augmented by a concatenation of solid-state devices. The theoretician's calling may seem to accord better with a high standard of personal convenience: his problems, and his solutions, are largely portable ones—how nice to be a mathematician waiting in an armchair, with a piece of paper, for an idea. As the scale of experiments, and especially of apparatus, grows larger, it becomes more imperative to rely on calculations in the early stages. It is extravagant to build a super-synchrotron as big as a battleship, only to discover that its performance is not quite as guessed, so that it will require the re-arrangement of a cruiserweight of iron to make the next approximation to the ideal. Something similar holds for loosely designed experiments, in which vast quantities of valueless data may be piled up if we have played fast and loose with the statistics.

So theory has its place. Yet the true scientific method is that everything should be brought to the test of experiment. The scalpel, even more than the pen, is mightier than the sword. If it be thought that scientific tradition need only receive passing thought in many practical situations of today, we may remember that, for unusual phenomena, there is always the danger that we will leave out a significant factor from our calculations. Of course, there is the parallel danger that we will have overlooked the fact that our experimental set-up is not representative in some respect, but it often seems possible to arrange matters experimentally so that we approach unquestionably close to the true state.

The most satisfying answer is the combination of theory and experiment. When both tell the same story, we can really believe it. Even when they contradict each other, it at least indicates something interesting for further study. So, even while he makes his measurements, the experimentalist should be feeling for a theory that will give them coherence; even while he calculates, the theoretician should be searching for observational checks that might be made. Sometimes there will be phases when what is observed baffles explanation. Then the only thing to do is to go on accumulating experimental results in the hope that some queer feature of them will give a clue to what lies behind. But that is a counsel of despair and it should always be accompanied by some puzzled groping after a way of explaining them. The only time when it is justified to make measurements without attempting to relate them to theoretical considerations is when it is perfectly clear what those considerations are, but the detailed application of them is more laborious than the direct experiment.

Thinking or acting

In many ways, making decisions when to act and when to think are a large part of the art of research. We do not mean that there should be any literally thoughtless acting. Rather are we trying to distinguish between the phase when all attention is concentrated on the technique employed at that moment—be it reading a meter, solving an equation or writing a paper—and the phase of stepping back from the work to examine it in its context on a larger or very large scale. There is a danger of spending too long thinking about the possibilities from a new experiment, and what we will do with the results when we have obtained them; perhaps another application comes to mind, so that we try a slightly different experiment before we have finished the first, only to interrupt that with a third. We, maybe, find most of them inconclusive and realise that we didn't know the errors involved anyhow, so we are left with no firm conclusions whatsoever that can be drawn. There is an opposite danger of consolidating each experiment so thoroughly that we move forward only at a very pedestrian rate.

A high power ultrasonic generator is a fascinating piece of equipment to be able to play with, especially when you have had no previous dealings with one. When our design—in the distant nineteen-forties—was at last working, the mound that it could throw up on the surface of irradiated water engaged our lively attention. An early thought was that surface tension must be tending to hold the mound down. So into the tank went a spoonful of liquid soap, in the hope that this would allow a much higher mound. But the mound completely disappeared. After—to our surprise—exonerating the generator from having broken down, we discovered that even a trace of soap made water highly absorbent of ultrasonics. This was a delightful demonstration to give our frequent visitors, but involved hard work cleaning out the tank again before the next demonstration. The solution was a small cell, to be placed in the path of the beam, that could have soap dripped into it and be more easily cleaned later. The final stage was when someone, trying this standard conjuring trick, reported that it would not work; it turned out that he had added an appreciable proportion of soap solution to the water, and we had the remarkable discovery that a few parts per million were highly absorbent, while a twenty per cent solution was not. The moral—though we have included the story more because it is a good story than because it has a moral!—is that sometimes you get most interesting results by rushing ahead with the experiment, but sometimes you need to sit back and think what it is all about.

Probability of an informative result

When we try to analyse more closely the thinking that leads to a decision whether or not to conduct a particular experiment (or embark on a particular line of calculation), we need to consider probabilities. One probability we must try to assess is that of achieving our objective. Another important probability to weigh up concerns the result of the experiment or calculation. Obviously, we cannot feel certain of the result, or we would not trouble to do the work. Perhaps the answer is a very open question (thinking of it, for simplicity, as a matter of Yes or No). Research programmes can go on usefully for a long time answering open questions. We may sometimes wonder why they have not been answered before: sometimes it will be because techniques have only recently become available that made it possible; often, especially in applied research, it will be simply because no one has bothered.

On the other hand, there is the occasional experiment that gives the completely unexpected answer. Of famous ones, we might quote work on electroscopes. Many people would have ignored the slow loss of charge from electroscopes as obviously due to leakage across the insulator or to ionisation from radioactive contaminants; they would have said that it was hardly worth going to much trouble to eliminate this leakage because it would obviously cure the trouble. But Hess' and others' insistence on checking the point gave the first evidence for cosmic rays, a subject that has grown to be almost a branch of science in its own right. Sometimes, no doubt, what was unexpected to the rest of the world was much less so to the scientist diligently studying the relevant field, and giving rein to his imagination. But often a chance observation will be rewarded, or the painstaking logging of results may lead through discrepancy to a discovery. So we have the nicely balanced choice between work that is sure to tell us something that is moderately interesting and work whose results will probably signify very little but may just possibly be very important; information theory can express this more precisely. The work we must avoid is that whose results have very little value whichever way they should turn out.

We must be particularly careful to avoid an uninformative experiment if it is costly or tedious to mount. In fact, the wise scientist is continually on the alert for experiments he can conduct easily. If little effort is demanded—perhaps because the equipment has previously been set up for another purpose—then 'long-shot' or even trivial experiments may be justified. By contrast, the very elaborate experiment should only be undertaken when its outcome is bound to have value, as a pointer to extensive subse-

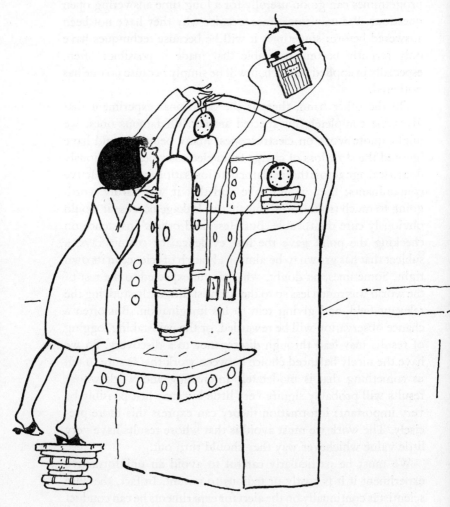

"The precise state of development of the apparatus"

quent work, or as that of an *experientia crucis* deciding unequivocally between rival theories.

Notebooks

Descending from the spacious realms of scientific strategy, from the large *How*? to the small, one of the bluntest of practical issues concerns the keeping of records. Schoolmasters may lay down rigid rules governing the precise upkeep of practical notebooks but for the real life of a research laboratory much less help is commonly given. It should be remembered that, as for report writing, notebook entries in schooldays and in researching days have little in common. The former are written for the pedagogue, to impress him with the writer's skill and orthodoxy; the latter are primarily for the writer's own benefit.

Human nature—at least, most humans' natures—will be tempted to skimp writing down the hour-by-hour progress of the experiment, but this is to mortgage future convenience and conviction for the fascination of the present. The precise state of development of the apparatus when a particular result was found, a full list of the simplifying assumptions made in the calculations, the purity of the constituents that the synthesis started from are all sure to be tantalisingly essential if they have not been recorded, and you will have the agonising decision whether or not to trust your memory a month or two later. Write it all down. A few may err to the other extreme—I recall one learned gentleman (now a Professor) saying of another (now only a Reader) that the comprehensiveness of his daily notebook must surely have made it include a record of the times at which he visited the toilet—but only a very few.

In what notebooks should this be done? I am a supporter of the two-notebook plan. Under this, there are two levels of recording. For the low book, anything goes; untidy scrawlings of figures, the ugliest of sketches, large empty spaces in tables that signify experiments abandoned as unfruitful alternating with gross overcrowding where the experiment was extended to cover a wider range of parameters' values. The only inescapable rule is that everything is written down. For the high book, the policy is the exact opposite. It is used much less frequently and everything entered there is inscribed with care. Selected extracts will be transferred from the low book, perhaps appearing for the first time in the right units, and will be freely interspersed with conclusions and proposals. Writing up the high book will essentially be a time for stock-taking, for thinking, for acting as a scientist.

There can be variations on this method. The low book should normally use only one side of the pages. The other side can then be used for occasional later additions and for those entries which you expect you will often want to refer to later and so to find more easily (more often than not, your expectations will be wrong, but they will be right sufficiently often to justify the operation!) Some people will think that judicious use of the blank pages will serve instead of a high book, especially if formal reports are issued at short intervals.

If several distinguishable themes are being pursued simultaneously—a rare, but not an impossible situation—there is an argument for several parallel notebooks. Arguments concerning economies, for this and for blank pages, should be put in their proper perspective, remembering that a successful research is worth—and costs—more than a warehouseful of books.

Graphs are probably best preserved in an independent book. Since every entry everywhere must be dated, cross referencing is simple. Where a variety of exotic scales are called for in the graphs, the situation is more complicated, and may warrant occasionally pasting sheets into another book.

Various alternative schemes for notebooks are acceptable. What all experienced research workers will agree on—at least, perverse creatures, until the maxim comes to be applied to themselves—is that loose pieces of paper are anathema. I am convinced of the soundness of this. Tear-off blocks should be banned from laboratories. It is so easy to scribble some readings on that loose sheet because you are doubtful whether they are worth taking; far too often, you will subsequently pass through the phases (in that order) when (*a*) you are convinced they were not worth taking and throw them away and (*b*) you realise that in some subtle respect they were invaluable and irreplaceable. The same thing holds for a multitude of oddly accumulated facts and jottings. Write them all down in a notebook. The humbler you are by temperament, the more you will need to convince yourself that even what even you have done needs to be preserved. In fact, my main purpose in down-grading the acceptance level for the quality of what appears in my low notebook is simply to remove the last vestige of excuse for not putting everything down in it.

We have suggested that the notebook is the hub from which referencing spokes go out to graphs. The same principle can hold for other, separately preserved (and, please, carefully indexed) records such as photographs. Data sheets are a special case—those pre-cast forms on which are entered vast lists of figures that describe an experiment. Do not be over-hasty to compile such a data sheet for printing. Most experiments can beneficially pass through the phase when what is happening is considered broadly before forcing the observations into the preordained pattern implied by a row of empty boxes waiting to be filled. The data sheet belongs with the phase when measurements have become routine and are passed to an assistant. One stage further is the print-out from the data-logger. Data-loggers are magnificent devices for accumulating vast stocks of figures with the minimum human toil (maintenance engineers excluded). They make possible many experiments which could not otherwise be done in a world from which slavery has been banished. But beware of the assumption that the logging of data is synonymous with research.

Apparatus

Any attempt to review, or even to list the range of equipment that is available, or that might be constructed to aid the researcher, would soon land us deep in the technicalities of the science under consideration. For apparatus is central to research. Yet there are some generalisations that can usefully be pondered, generalisations that concern the scientist's attitude to his equipment, rather than particular features of specific examples.

To make or to buy is the first question that must be answered. Extreme factors, such as a deficiency of cash or a deficiency of constructors may settle this issue. If it is still an open one, a first approximation is that bought equipment is nearly always cheaper under a just system of accounting; the economies of quantity production normally outweigh the profit that is extracted, and even if it is a one-off item of manufacture, the facilities commonly available, if the right supplier has been approached, will often reduce the real price of the bought job below its do-it-yourself equivalent. But there are arguments in the opposite direction. Firstly, some constructional services will have to be provided in all laboratories for cases where outside manufacture just is not feasible—notably because design modifications are likely to arise all along the line of development. The workshop will then comprise a facility that can only vary slowly in capacity, but has to be matched to a load that is sure to be fluctuating wildly. This must lead to occasions when the facility is relatively lightly loaded and on these occasions it will be sound policy to feed in work whose acceptance would not normally be justified. Secondly, and more subtly, is the effect on the research worker. If the habit is too firmly engrained in him of acquiring all his gear remotely ready-made, there will be a danger of his not appreciating its limitations; he will tend to accept at its face value every index on the scale that his pointer points to and every datum that his logger has logged. Moreover, he will find it much harder to visualise how easily or otherwise the capabilities of his apparatus could be extended in any given direction, and this will handicap him in planning the next stage of his research. Thirdly, it is a woefully common experience that equipment constructed externally takes a distressingly long time to make.

If the equipment should be bought ready-made, then it will often be wise for the user to make a definite effort to understand it—in some of its practical details, as well as its fundamental principles. This will prevent him from being too much at the mercy of the manufacturer—or even at that of the manufacturer's contact man, in the shape of the local instrument engineer. But there is an opposite extreme. For a few people it may be right that they should master all the intricacies of electronics—it is nearly always electronics that is involved nowadays—and become instrumentation experts. But for some, to go far in that direction would leave them too little time to be users; they must put some faith in their advisers, trusting them in particular to say when the equipment they have provided can not be trusted.

The principles governing the design of your apparatus will be found in the text books relating to your subject. What they are not likely to emphasise is that when you are trying out a new idea, your equipment should be as simple as possible, so that a principle can be established without having to wait through the long preludes while non-essential complications are made to function. Concentrate on doing only one difficult thing at a time. Refinements may one day be imperative, but leave them to the later stage—which may never arise, if the principle is disproved in the first stage. This, of course, is just another facet of the tactics of research we have discoursed on earlier.

The text-books are also likely to omit any mention of the need for flexibility (of the metaphorical type) in your early prototypes. It requires exceptional foresight to anticipate all the ways in which you will want to modify and distort the gear to accommodate later experiments, so leave it as open as possible for changes to be introduced without scrapping large sections of the apparatus. Never, for instance, allow your workshop to weld anything together; they will want to, for it is a simple operation, but invariably it is just at that particular joint that you will want to alter the structure—easy if bolted, impossible if welded. To combine simplicity with flexibility is, of course, very difficult. It requires thought. That is where the art of designing research equipment comes in.

Very often, it will be found that there are two distinct phases that apparatus passes through. At first, a crude early model, possessing only the bare essential features, allows the pioneer experiments to be done. Experience with this—bitter experience of the delays it involves, and of the patience needed to coax it into performing—leads to the design of a streamlined version with which more accurate results can be obtained predictably and more quickly even by less skilled personnel. It must be realised that, if the basic idea is sound enough to have a long life, later generations of equipment will be almost unrecognisably unlike their early precursors. Incidentally, thinking backwards, it should similarly be remembered how very primitive were the early devices which bore the same name as their modern counterparts, and consequently how heroic were the experimenters who succeeded in wringing results out of them—I think I remember Moseley, of X-Ray spectral fame, being instanced as one who would work, almost with his finger stopping up the leak, under vacuum conditions that the mildest technician of today would regard as quite intolerable.

We have indicated that for the first experiments of a type the simplest possible equipment ought often to be cudgelled into doing duty. On the other hand, when apparatus, whether instruments or process plant, is to leave the shelter of a laboratory and face the wintry climate of the world outside, it is essential, as we have already urged (p. 42) that it should possess a high degree, not of sophistication, but of robustness and reliability.

Errors

For a book that sets out to be general and human, descriptive rather than mathematical, the subject of errors is getting dangerously technical. Probably it is a technicality that most research workers would benefit from studying, but we will not venture here into the mathematics of probability or the defects inherent in particular mechanisms. There is still something to be usefully said about the scientist's attitude to the errors he may be making.

Primarily, this is to urge again the need for the scepticism and self-examination that we have commended before. Let every link in the chain of measurement—or of reasoning—be scrutinised. Not that it must be discarded if less than perfect: it would be an extravagance to have constructed a system approaching perfection. But there should never be an easy optimism of blindly hoping that something is adequate and then dismissing it from thought. The accepted limitation—yes, often; the calculated risk—yes, sometimes. But not unthinking ignorance. To augment the mental patrol, inspecting the errors of every contributory item, the exercise of imaginative anticipation is often helpful. Picture yourself getting an unexpected result, first in one way then in the other; often you will find your immediate reaction is to think that it must be the whatsit playing you up, and if you have appreciated this beforehand you may be able to take steps to improve the whatsit's performance.

In the design of indicating and control systems, increasing attention is currently being paid to problems of making apparatus 'fail-safe'. When an instrumentation system is monitoring a process that can reach a dangerous situation, it is obviously less disastrous for errors to lead to safe conditions being shown as dangerous (a 'fail-safe' failure) than *vice versa*. There is an analogy in scientific experiments. If a fault spoils the experiment, so that no results accrue at all, that is fail-safe. If the error produces incorrect results, that is dangerous. In designing an experiment and considering its weaknesses, these two eventualities should be clearly distinguished and wherever possible the former should be chosen.

Sometimes we find the situation where some factor is known to be, in principle, a source of error, but it cannot easily be determined whether the magnitude of the error is significant. It is often possible and useful, then, to increase the factor deliberately (even though it cannot be reduced) and observe whether sensibly the same result is obtained. If increasing the factor—and therefore presumably worsening the error—has not affected the result, the two, identical answers can generally be taken as valid. A slight danger to be alert to is a non-linear relation between factor and error; in particular, any saturation mechanism can mean that although the error has not been increased in the second case it was present equally in both cases.

A sound instinct to cultivate is that of always conducting an experiment in the minimum reasonable time ('reasonable' of course excludes undue haste: we are really just trying to eliminate dawdling). Most experiments amount to a comparison between two or more different states, and this favouring of swift working amounts to an attempt to minimise the effects of uncontrollable variables, such as slowly drifting temperatures. More precisely, we could talk of any disturbance, or 'noise' making the experiment less precise. The noise will often have components at many frequencies and by reducing the time spanned by our experiment we can eliminate the effect of the components of lowest frequency. Such concepts lead into the recognition of errors as either random or systematic, the former corresponding to 'noise' and the latter to permanent faults such as mistaken calibrations. It is wise to begin to understand such analysis. It is dangerous to allow it to make us lose sight of realities. Blackett quotes the—possibly apochryphal—story of Rutherford saying: 'Do forget about the theory of errors and go back to your laboratory and do the experiment again'*. Indeed, most of the concept of statistical significance is just the same as the old-fashioned idea: do we expect to find the same result in a repeat experiment?

In general it will be found that the most convincing experiments for demonstrating cause and effect are those in which it has been contrived that a single factor is changed with a consequent direct change in some other quantity that is being measured. On the other hand, statisticians are loud in their insistence that, in appropriate cases, a suitably designed set of experiments can give simultaneous information about the effects of many factors.

---

* P. M. S. BLACKETT, Rutherford Memorial Lecture, 1954, *Year Book of the Physical Society*, 1955, p. 19.

These considerations of errors are primarily applicable to experimental work, but corresponding issues arise on the theoretical side. Tools of the trade, of course, are increasingly used in that trade, in the shape of computers. A passing thought might be spared for their failings. Some special purpose analogue models may produce misleading results. On the whole, however, fail-safe systems have been achieved, in that computer failures will lead to idle time, while the apparatus is out of service, but are hardly likely to produce false readings capable of slipping through the net of self-checks that has been spread for them.

Errors in theory are more likely to arise on the human side. Possibly the mathematics is faulty. More likely is it that the mathematical "model" depicting the physical situation will be incorrect. This is an especial danger if the model is constructed jointly by a mathematician and another scientist much less skilled in that field; for there may be a failure to understand each other so that the interlingual translation is not carried out faithfully.

There is almost always the risk of error because simplifications have been introduced. Real life is invariably complex (scientifically, as well as in human situations!). Simple things like vacua and pure materials are difficult and expensive to come by, increasingly so as they approach the absolute. Therefore if any handleable mathematical representation is to be made, it must omit many factors which have a finite but small influence. A simplified and therefore erroneous model must be used. Just as in the experimental case, these sources of error should be considered one by one; judgment must be exercised, so that those which are trivial can be briefly dismissed, while those that are larger or less easily assessed receive appropriately more extensive treatment. An interplay between calculation and experiment may be desirable on both sides; some experimental errors will be measured and some calculated, while theoretical shortcomings can similarly be assessed sometimes on paper and sometimes by suitable observations.

Assistants

It might be expected that assistants should feature in the *Who?* chapter, as essential characters in the cast of the research drama. But what we are really discussing is *how* to use them, so that this is the more appropriate place. For the role of the scientific assistant—or whatever his title may be at the laboratory in question —is a useful parameter by which to distinguish different stages of the work. Most scientists dream of having more helpers to help them than are actually available at the moment of dreaming. More often than not, their dream is soundly based—probably because the conservatism of management makes it think in terms of a decade or two ago, when equipment was so much simpler that it was better operated by the scientist himself—but not always.

When a new graduate starts in the real world of research, and sometimes when a more senior man starts in a new field, it is desirable for him to do rather more of the donkey work than his sense of self-importance would welcome. In this way he will learn more soundly the details, the limitations and the possibilities of his tools. Later, he can then more safely delegate. This principle can be enlarged upon to indicate the general desirable procedure for experimenting.

Sometimes, a long series of experiments can be planned, for which the framework is perfectly clear. A defined set of actions must be gone through, conscientiously and deliberately, and it is known in advance what will happen, except for the exact readings indicated on certain dials. The experimental results are contained in them (or if the experimenter is up-to-date and labour-saving minded, in the recorders—preferably digital—connected to them). In these circumstances, it is sound to delegate the conduct of the experiment to an assistant. If a degree of manual dexterity is called for, he will very likely put up a better performance than his scientist master.

But when the outcome of the experiment is more in doubt, it is important that the man inherently responsible should be present. Especially is this so when ignorance is *qualitative*—when we don't know *what* will happen. Even when the ignorance is *quantitative*, with wide bounds—we have very little idea how much will happen—first-hand observation is very desirable. This is the way that extra insight comes; this is in the true scientific tradition of observing and deducing.

Another situation calls for the presence of the scientist who has designed the experiment. This is when he is aiming to save time by allowing the result of the first experiment to decide what the second experiment shall be, and so on. This is a dangerous procedure—but that does not mean it should never be followed. It involves the risk of some uncertainty creeping in, or some misjudgment, so that in the end there are no solid results that can be relied on at all. But it also has the possibility of great time saving, compared with the conscientious completion of a comprehensive set of pre-planned measurements, many of which are later realised to be irrelevant. It seems probable that this sort of technique is often the way in which the really talented man soars ahead of his slower competitors. In principle, all the permutations of results of earlier experiments could be tabulated with the consequent courses to be followed, and the instructions could be passed to the assistant for implementing. But in complex situations, the scientist would be even more of a genius if he did not overlook something, while the assistant capable of carrying it all out could well be promoted to be an experimenter in his own right.

Situations demanding the presence of the responsible scientist occur most frequently near the beginning of work with a novel flavour. They arise particularly at the stage of commissioning new apparatus, when the '*experiment*' is aimed at demonstrating that performance and specification bear some resemblance to each other.

Whether or not we are trying to cut corners by making last-minute decisions over experiments, it is always sound to think ahead, as though science were a game of chess with Nature, in which we must anticipate her next move, and, as far as possible, counter it in advance. We repeat from an earlier section the advice

"Red herrings and wild geese"

that the failure of equipment should always be imagined as vividly as possible, because when the catastrophe has really overtaken us, we invariably gain a clarity of vision that suggests several avenues to try, any of which may throw light on, or correct the defect.

Similarly, we should always be thinking at least one jump ahead, asking ourselves (I remember Prof.—later Sir Charles— Ellis expounding along these lines) what conclusions we could draw if the experimental results turned out in such-and-such a way. And if we find that we would be saying '*So what?*' it is probably a bad experiment, which we could save time by not doing.

Red herrings and wild geese

An important question that arises from time to time (not only for zoologists) is whether or not various projects and sub-projects that propose themselves are to be classified as these notorious fish or birds whose pursuit never achieves its goal. Sometimes in every live laboratory ideas will be generated that have part of their origin in the main research work but do not immediately serve to further it directly*. At the purest end of research, it may be a chance observation or something unexpected: no firm conclusions can be drawn from that single, isolated event, but if it were repeated in more precisely defined conditions it might open up an intriguing field. A new way of thinking about a problem, developed to analyse one particular situation, shows promise of fruitful results if applied to different, but related problems; for instance, the electronic engineer may analyse his circuit sufficiently to reach its own optimum and then realise that a little further work might generalise the solution into a form that he could leave neatly concluded for posterity. An instrument designed for one purpose may suggest principles that could be

---

* W. I. B. BEVERIDGE, *The Art of Scientific Investigation*, 3rd ed., Heinemann, London, 1957, p. 36.

applied to another. As a small example, I recall investigating the attenuation of an alternating magnetic field, passing through sheet metal, as a means of determining thickness. Studying the end effect, to see how closely the edge could be approached without anomalies, revealed, with certain configurations, an unexpectedly sharp change. This prompted diversion of effort to study how electro-magnetic screening could be used to determine the position of an edge and, as it has worked out, the latter application has been used much more widely than the former.

So that such opportunities will most likely arise at one time or another. Should they be taken? We suggest that they should seldom, if ever, be taken immediately. If the original work is abandoned precipitately, its value will largely be lost, whereas a rounding off to whatever stage has nearly been reached will preserve at least something from it. Again, too frequent and too rapid changes of direction introduce an unsettling atmosphere into a laboratory. While, not least, an interval to gain perspective nearly always allows a better judgment to be made of the value of the new proposal that has cropped up; and good ideas do not deteriorate during brief storage.

On the other hand, there are sound arguments in favour of pursuing novelties—after a decent interval. It is good for morale, in that research workers feel that they are engaged on something of their very own, right from the basic conception. History would probably indicate that many of the most fruitful lines of development had started in this way.

The extent to which red herrings can be pursued must vary according to the type of laboratory worked in. Where the most fundamental work is done, it will be reasonable to go off after new targets—lack of them may even be taken as an indication of sterility. There will be a restriction if the original research depends on very expensive apparatus; it would be tactless to abandon this prematurely, or to alter drastically a programme of shared work affecting many people. Laboratories with more emphasis on applied work will probably have the direction of their labours more closely controlled, so that, unless the red herring merely constitutes a different route to the same objective, it will be more difficult to follow it up: at the least, a longer interval is likely before a new project can be launched, and then it will probably have to be done less casually.

In any event, of course, skilled judgment is called for to assess, with the appropriate weightings for or against novelty, whether the new line is more worth following than the old. Again, as so often in this chapter, we come up against the need for judgment. This is why there is so much art inextricably engrained in research work. In strategy and tactics an indefinable creative ability is wanted, that will draw on the stored skill of the subconscious to make decisions about what line of work to follow. Such decisions are often more far-reaching than the simpler logical exercises associated with the scientific work itself.

6. Why?

Why should I be as one that turneth aside?
Song of Solomon 1:7.

Why why?

'*Why*? is of course the most profound question of all, at least if it is taken to its deeper levels. There are different levels, just because the answers to *Why*? can often be given in alternative ways. Sometimes these can be distinguished by whether they describe prime causes or immediate causes, but the analysis in terms of immediacy does not always seem the most helpful. There is, for instance, a distinction between the occasions when the question '*why*?' could be expanded into: 'What is the historical sequence leading up to the situation?' and those when it is an abbreviation for 'What is the moral obligation behind the action?'

Clever parents, of course, have for long realised the multiplicity of true answers to specific why's and have often used it to prevent the barrage of their offspring's questions from leading them into embarrassing corners. If asked, for instance, why there are so many weeds on the flower beds, a botany lesson will be just as truthful and relevant as an admission that father has been dozing in the deck-chair all week-end. A homily starting from Genesis 3:18 would be a third possible reply in a third dimension.

So it will not be surprising if several different, but not mutually exclusive answers can be given to the question: '*Why do research*?'

132

National need

We can start from a national viewpoint. Our question is then tantamount to asking how it comes about that Britain's (or many other countries') best interests are served through her citizens' pursuit of research. Some readers may be scornful of a very amateur economist's analysis, but it does not need a deep survey to realise not only the desirability but the grim necessity of research. If goods are to be sold in competitive world markets, they must have merits over their rivals, that is, must be in some respects better value. (Apart, that is, from such distortions of the true merit order as can be procured by advertising!) Now the classical factors of capital and labour, employed to give anything produced its value, should really be thought of nowadays as needing a third ingredient, namely technical skill. A shortfall in any of these factors must be compensated by an increase in the others. But we have no capital to spare, and to increase our labour would be to depress our inviolable standards of living. So only technical skill is left. And that is closely bound up with research.

Put in other words, we are blessed with few natural resources or international vantage points. One of our few raw materials is native ingenuity, and woe betide us if we do not exploit it—it has the great advantage that it can be the reverse of a diminishing asset. But the world does not wait for us: technical innovations are made elsewhere if they are not thought of here, and yesterday's processes very rapidly become obsolete and uneconomic. Therefore, it is, industrially, truer than we may care to think to say that we research or perish.

Priority for technology

The research that is economically necessary, however, is well out towards the development end of the spectrum (of Fig. 1). It is more difficult to justify more fundamental research on a strictly financial basis. Knowledge of basic scientific facts must tend to be shared world-widely. Admittedly, there is some force

in the argument that those who have been involved in fundamen-
al discoveries—or their close colleagues—will be best equipped
to follow up the discoveries in practical applications; but if there
is a shortage of trained man-power—and there is—the end where
economies can be effected is the fundamental end. It is possible
for industry to get such basic science second-hand; it is impossible
for it to get its detailed technology second-hand without becoming subservient to the concern from which it gets it. We would
therefore repeat the warnings that have been given in many quar-
ters of the national danger that is inherent in our present tendency
to emphasise the pure and the academic at the expense of the
applied and the technological*.

It would be possible to err towards the other extreme. A
national research programme that was all engineering and development would have cut off the invigoration that comes with
the radical ideas of revolutionary research. The liveliness of
teaching would be reduced if it were all removed from association
with the inspiration of fundamental new discovery—the aca-
demics may tend to over-emphasise this, but there is certainly
some truth in the idea. It would—and this is the deepest objection
—be opting out of one of the richest streams of human intellectual activity.

Although the fortunes of science and technology are inter-
woven in many ways, the two are ultimately incommensurable,
and the choice between them cannot be made on strictly rational
grounds. Broadly speaking, technology will be supported for the
contribution it makes to material wellbeing, pure science because of its idealistic significance and its cultural importance. It
may well be doubted whether, in this country, the proportioning
of effort between science and technology has actually come about
through anyone's dispassionate appraisal. Rather does it seem

---

* *Annual Report of the Advisory Council on Scientific Policy*, 1963–1964,
H.M.S.O.,London, 1964, 48 pp.
C. F. CARTER, Government and Technology, *Nature*, 206 (1965) 652–
654.

to be the product of a large number of independent, short-range forces, each exercising an unco-ordinated influence upon society. In a number of contexts, we may well ask: why science? and why not technology?

Personal Why?s

In this book, however, we are more concerned with matters from the personal, individual point of view—sniping only occasionally at issues of large-scale social significance! There are still many why?s on the personal level. If you are trying to find the way a man thinks, you will repeatedly ask him: Why this? why that?—of course, for then he will tell you his *reasons* and *reasoning* is a very important activity. At the shallow end, Why? shades off into How? The answer to the question of *why* I wear an overcoat is only another way into the problem of *how* I keep warm in the winter. But at the deep end, to ask: 'Why do such-and-such research in such-and-such a way?' is to probe right down to fundamentals.

Motivation

It may be doubted whether there is a unique answer to the question whether research workers need an overall motivation before they can do good work. In general it is recognised that men perform more effectively when supported by an appreciation of where they fit into the scheme of things: there were stories of war-time factories whose productivity soared when trouble was taken to explain to the folk at the benches just how their products were of value to the troops. It might be expected that scientific research, with its need for a creative approach, would be particularly dependant on temperament and temper, and therefore sensitive to a sound motivational basis. While some scientists will doubtless feel the need to carry their logical study of problems as far back as they can to an overall justification for the field of their labours, general observation suggests that for the majority this is not so. For instance, the fact that an individual is concerned with the development of nuclear armaments does not necessarily mean that he has carefully thought out all the international and ethical implications and reached a satisfactory conclusion. In this and other matters, it is dangerously easy to think little and lightly, to rationalise, and to dismiss from our minds. We in Britain criticise the German technologists who were so absorbed in their laboratories that they left their politicians to keep their political consciences. We may point out how the Russian ignores the incompatibility between the freedom of science and the dogma of Marx which his political commissar proclaims. But, in so doing, we may be throwing stones from glassier houses than we realise.

If sociological justification is sometimes not necessary for them, why in fact do scientists continue faithfully with their work? Partly, no doubt, just from force of habit and following the line of least resistance. A university faculty has been chosen because it accorded best with the examination results that happened to fall out; university teaching was geared to a subsequent career in research, so it naturally came about that the science graduate was swept into the research world; which entered, a firm resolution would be needed to escape from it.

Personal satisfactions

But there are very real, very strong attractions and satisfactions in the world of research. There is a camaraderie of the laboratory that is, perhaps, not quite paralleled anywhere else. Maybe it comes because there you have comparatively clever men rubbing shoulders in their ordinary work-a-day activities, whereas in most organisations many of the folk of graduate status have their day-to-day contacts mainly with their juniors, meeting their equals only seldom and then often as rivals. Maybe the right pressure to work is important and in a good laboratory a middle way can be followed between the clamour of successive emergencies that must be met and the torpor of trivial routine. Men always seem to work together better when united by a common foe—and it is healthier for this foe to be a Nature reluctant to yield her secrets or a technology that will not be tamed, rather than a human adversary. (It has been said in laboratory circles that the administrators—the scientist's natural enemies and predators—fulfil a useful function also in providing a common hate-figure with all the unifying stimulus that brings!)

Related to the satisfaction of the lab. camaraderie is the respect of his peers, which a scientist can rightly enjoy. While many people would scorn the unthinking adulation of those not in a position to judge, the very objectivity of science makes it possible for a small circle—or, occasionally, a larger one—to appreciate unreservedly a good piece of work that has been accomplished; the consciousness of this is undoubtedly one of the rewards compensating for the ardours of research.

Achievement of a goal

Quite apart from appreciation by colleagues or acquaintances, there is always a personal satisfaction in achieving a goal. Presumably this comes to the businessman who has built up an enterprise or to the politician who has achieved power and used it to bring about long sought ends. It must be a large part of the reward of the creative artist. To the scientist, no less, there is a lasting satisfaction in a problem solved. It may be the theoretical explanation of observations in terms of known or novel concepts. It may be apparatus performing some function that was previously unknown. It may be merely some measurements never made before: perhaps no great significance will ever be attached to the values that have emerged, but their very absence was a challenge that has been met and mastered. As Mount Everest, in Mallory's words, had to be climbed just because it was there, so a scientific problem that has been posed must be solved and with its solution comes a surprising intellectual reward. Moreover, such rewards are not only for the great. Of course, there must be the greatest satisfaction in producing an answer that has escaped the world's whole scientific fraternity for years. But in every laboratory, problems arise in particular circumstances that call for particular technical solutions.

To some extent, no doubt, this is true in any career, but the continuous outreach of science imparts an essential novelty even to her day-to-day problems. They may not have the human interest associated with ordering the affairs of men, but there will be a greater objectivity than is found in problems arising from the unpredictability of people.

Scientific curiosity

One pleasure that cannot occur so often in other professions is simply that of satisfying curiosity. When we are young, we are possessed of a refreshing zeal to find out all sorts of things that we do not know. Alas, with age comes a tendency to leave behind the 'satiable curiosity of the Elephant Child, and to substitute for it the laziness of an unquestioning acceptance; but some curiosity persists with all of us, and one of the quiet joys of the laboratory is to have it satisfied when some problem that has baffled us is finally solved. Of course, the thoughtful scholar of any subject can experience this as new understanding comes to him, but he is often treading in other people's footsteps. The scientist, particularly, can occasionally feel that he is satisfying the restless curiosity of all his fellows. In fact, this sense of playing a part in the continuous, world-wide expansion of knowledge has itself a strong attraction. The idea of science growing slowly but inexorably, and of our sharing in this, can catch our imaginations.

Technology and human welfare

For those on the applied side of research, there is a close equivalent in joining in the progressive mastery of Nature. Partly, this is again just the challenge of problems waiting to be solved. Also, although we have suggested that not all technologists will trouble to analyse the basis of their work to this extent, they can, in fact, often draw satisfaction from their promotion of the welfare of humanity: their problem may be, not only an intellectual riddle, but a challenge to human compassion.

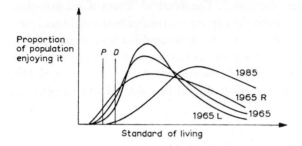

Fig. 13. Distribution of different standards of living.

The latter can be most marked, no doubt, on the medical side, when no imagination is needed to realise the benefits that can be brought. A short step extends the field to agricultural and food research, and a slightly longer step extends it to almost any industry that can contribute to raised living standards. It may be worth a brief diversion to enquire how far into the future this second extension will continue to be justified as an obvious philanthropic exercise. The standards enjoyed by a community can be considered very broadly as a whole; an overall increase can therefore be seen to improve the situation for needy cases, even though we may have reservations about the desirability of increased luxury for cases that are already well favoured. The relative distribution of wealth, and whether or not it should be altered, is a separate issue. But if we now look carefully and far ahead, a different situation can be foreseen. The line 1965 in Fig. 13 represents the current distribution of living standards, D and P indicating the levels below which discomfort and poverty respectively appear. Political action to left or right might change the shape or the curve to 1965L or 1965R, but economic forces might prevent changes beyond the former, which still includes a finite area under the curve and to the left of D. It should be noted that for a given population both the area under the curve, and (for a given consumed production) the abscissa of its centroid are fixed. With technological growth, however, we can look forward to a curve 1985, with only a very small hard core of poverty or even discomfort. The worthwhileness of technological development to push the curve even further to the right will then call for much more searching re-examination. Many people would say that if curve 1985 held for an advanced country, while those for underdeveloped countries were still far away to the left, the bulk of research effort should be oriented to changing the latter.

The philosophy of the desirable

These are some of the things suggested by a rather brief analysis as proving rewarding in the research worker's life. As a matter of observation, they are reasons why—for some people—it is good to do research. If we try to go one stage deeper and ask why these experiences should bring satisfaction, we are in greater difficulty. We may say that they contribute to the good life but what we mean by the good life must depend on our philosophy. To the Christian, they appear consistent with his all-embracing, if dimly comprehended, world-view. As the artist and musician of a pre-scientific culture tried to glorify God in the beauty of their art, so the scientist can reveal another facet of His glory in the beauty of scientific order. As man is made in the image of God, his welfare should be promoted and Nature subjected to him. So the superstructure is related back to the axiom. The Humanist has his dogma of the value of mankind, but it seems difficult to escape the conclusion that what he regards as good for mankind is ultimately a matter of each individual's opinion. In the field of elementary welfare, of course, there will be little argument: health, education, adequate leisure, for instance, will be universally acceptable as targets. But as the scope of what is technologically possible widens, there may be deeper differences over the ends to be aimed at. Will there ever be a clash between the promotion of intelligence and the promotion of unselfishness? Have the clever an inherent right to authority over the dull? Does human nature need opportunities for service and even sacrifice if it is to achieve its full stature? And so on.

So that *Why?* and its supplementaries can and should take us out into the deeper water of questioning.

Bibliography

A number of references have already been given as footnotes, when there was a direct connection with part of our text. The following list, partly overlapping the footnotes, is of publications with a general relevance to our subject.

J. D. BERNAL, *The Social Function of Science*, Routledge, London, 1939, 482 pp.

P. FREEDMAN, *The Principles of Scientific Research*, Macdonald, London, 1949, 222 pp.

W. I. B. BEVERIDGE, *The Art of Scientific Investigation*, 3rd ed., Heinemann, London, 1957, 178 pp.

J. JEWKES *et al.*, *The Sources of Invention*, Macmillan, London, 1958, 428 pp.

LINDOR BROWN, *The Perils of Leadership in Science*, Oxford University Press, London, 1960, 20 pp.

I. W. WARK, *Scientific Research as a Career*, Nature, 197 (1963) 737–740.

S. RAPPORT AND H. WRIGHT (Eds.), *Science: Method and Meaning*, New York University Press, New York, 1963, 258 pp.
(This is a series of reprints of articles, ranging at least from 1909 to 1958)

S. TOULMIN, *Foresight and Understanding*, Hutchinson, London, 1961, 115 pp.

D. EDGE (Ed.), *Experiment*, British Broadcasting Corporation, London, 1964, 71 pp.